I GOT ISSUES

Finding Purpose after Your Pieces

LATONYA M. WHITEHEAD

IN MEMORY OF

"GRANNY"
Frances Jean McBride
December 3, 1935 - September 9, 2021

"BIG MAMA"
Lillie Bell McCall
November 18, 1917- December 28, 2009

"UNCLE CARL"
Carl Anthony McCurdy
July 4, 1961 - February 23, 2003

"CHRISSY"
Christine D. Denson
January 20, 1977- September 17, 2000

"PAPA"
Lawyer McBride
April 16, 1934 - November 18, 1999

"BIG MA"
ZANNIE O'NEAL
August 12,1906- September 30, 1983

"MADEAR"
JEANETTE O'NEAL
May 27, 1935- November 11, 1981

Names of some persons mentioned in this book have been modified to protect the character and their reputation in conjunction with the book's sensitive subject matter.

ACKNOWLEDGEMENTS

I would like to thank my Lord and Savior Jesus Christ, for dying on the cross for my sins, so that I may have an opportunity to live for him and pursue his purpose for my life.

To my husband, David Duane Whitehead Sr., Thank you so much for being patient with me throughout my growing processes; I know we have endured challenging times; you trusted this vision and motivated me to continue writing! I really appreciate it; I Love you!

To my three wonderful children, Jarred, Jazmine, and J'Kala, I would like to thank you for staying in the fight with me. We faced some really hard times together. You believed me when I said, "we are all we got!" I wouldn't trade one moment for the times we've shared. You are forever my heart... I love you and I have no favorites!

To my mother, Debra Parker, it has never mattered how we started, but what is most important, is how we finished! I've always desired to make you proud mama. I love you so much, I am a replica of you- tough on the surface, soft on the inside and built to last in spite of! I am your daughter, you pushed and I became!

To my family and readers of this book, I thank you for trusting in the book's cover in hopes that it does what is intended for it. Thank you for taking the time to read my story, as I purposely, with passion, allow God to use my story of transparency to help heal others.

To my dad, George A. Williams, without you, there would be no me. I am so proud of you Pops! You survived what killed many others. All Praises to God, the Father, The Son, and the Holy Spirit.

Leonard Payton, you are awesome, you stepped in right on time. You were the presence needed in our home. Though there was separation, there was always a bond. I am forever, your one and only daughter!

To Angela Williams, it has been forty years plus and you have remained the same caring, loving woman from the first day I met you. You have always acknowledged me as your daughter, Thank You Neicy, you were sometimes the last one standing next to me when all others had given up on me. "I Love you so much!"

To you Miss Mamie McCarty- My dear friend, my God Mother, my counselor, my so many things. You were there always siding with me but being candid and honest enough to tell me the truth. I speak healing over your life – in the name of Jesus! Thank you for loving me- "your little girl!"

To my grandchildren, I have a prayed over each of you, asking God to bless you by showing you your purpose. I hope that you never wander in the wilderness carrying hereditary patterns of your predecessors. Allow this book to motivate you and transform you by using my life as your cheat sheet. – With the greatest love- Your Nana

To my dear nieces and nephews, you all have the opportunity to give life your best shots. You truly can have what you say and be who you want when you take on the challenge. I believe in you! I know you can do it! Much Love Nana

FOREWORD

LaTonya has always believed that her life is an open book. That's why she's sharing her story in this book. Some may question her decision to reveal so much about herself, but her motivation is simple: she wants to help others. She wants to inspire others to overcome obstacles, alleviate their suffering, and make a meaningful impact on their lives. LaTonya's passion for helping others has led her to start a movement, guided by her faith in God.

In this nonfiction story, LaTonya candidly shares her life story, starting with her adolescence as a teenage track runner. She describes how her running pattern, from the two to four-hundred-meter sprints, mirrored her life as she ignored warning signs, relied on others to fix her mistakes, and persevered through difficult times. Despite the curves and hurdles she faced, she remained focused and determined to reach her ultimate goal. The story ultimately concludes with her reaching her purpose and finishing the race.

LaTonya was born to George and Debra, who were both teenagers when they married with the consent of their parents. However, they divorced before LaTonya was two years old. From the moment she was born, her great-grandparents, John and Martha Sigmon, prayed for her protection and a life devoted to God. Unfortunately, Martha passed away 11 days later and John died four months after. Despite this, all of LaTonya's grandparents were devout Christians who covered her in prayer.

Her mother, who was also raised in church, was advised by many members to give her up for adoption, but she couldn't imagine her life without her daughter. To provide for her family, she lied about her age to find employment and eventually put herself through college to become a nurse at the age of 25. However, her busy schedule meant that she missed many of LaTonya's events and activities during her preteens and teenage years. She focused solely on providing for them and giving her the best life, she could, not realizing that LaTonya also needed her attention and affection. As LaTonya became a rebellious teenager and young woman, her mother had to let go and trust in God.

As you read LaTonya's story, her mother hopes that you will benefit from seeing the challenges she faced and her trust in God to overcome them. You will also see the rough patches and tough love between mother and daughter, neglect, abandonment, divorce, abuse, and backsliding from God. LaTonya's hope is that this story will help anyone with similar issues by trusting in God and having faith through his grace and mercy.

Thank You Lord Jesus for your Grace and Mercy

Debra S. Parker

CONTENTS

INTRODUCTION   1

CHAPTER 1   5

What Just Happened

CHAPTER 2   12

Speak Up, Say Something

CHAPTER 3   21

The Big Cat-Fish

CHAPTER 4   32

Baby on Board

CHAPTER 5   40

The Bus Stops Here

CHAPTER 6   49

Keep your Foot on the Gas

CHAPTER 7   58

Don't Lose Your Strength

CHAPTER 8   65

The Stranger in My House

CHAPTER 9   81

Life After Death

CHAPTER 10   95

Pick a Side

CHAPTER 11   112

Make Something Happen

CHAPTER 12   120

The Cheat Sheet

CHAPTER 13   138

I am that Dummy

CHAPTER 14   149

Identity Theft

INTRODUCTION

Being too young to attend school, I sat on my grandmother's couch, playing with my doll; with my five-year-old fingers sliding down the back, to the top helm of my shorts, while sitting that day, pulling off the white creamy stuff that rested on my back, smelling like nothing I had ever smelled; not knowing what it was but easily able to recognize the stuff on my fingers infiltrated me, taking a piece of my childhood with it.

My uncle Steven came home from school and found me sitting on the couch, playing with an unknown substance on my fingers. He asked me what it was and I told him I didn't know. He asked me several more times and I could tell he knew what it was, but I didn't. Eventually, he took me to my grandmother, who was in the kitchen, and explained the situation to her. I don't remember the exact words he used to describe the strange, faint-smelling, white, thick, gooey substance that was now dissolving into my skin.

My grandmother asked me, "Tonya, what is that? What happened? Where did you get it?" I felt a knot in my stomach and avoided eye contact, knowing I had done something wrong. I began to tell her the story of one of the nightmares that has haunted me for years.

At age five, I loved putting together jigsaw puzzles and playing with my dolls. I would dress them up and comb their hair. One day, while I was sitting alone on the couch combing my dolls' hair, my Uncle Charlie entered the room and asked me, "Do you want to come into my room and comb my hair?" Excitedly, I jumped off the couch to honor his request. My Uncle Charlie had a huge head of hair, so I couldn't resist the opportunity to play with it, especially since it was an afro.

Once he entered his room, he lay flat on his stomach on the bed. I remember the huge iron bed with head and foot boards resembling rusty prison bars, and I had to use the side rails to climb onto it. Uncle Charlie then instructed me to sit on his back and comb his hair. I combed and combed, attempting to section his hair into parts and pretending I could plait or braid it. Then, Uncle Charlie began to maneuver, rolling over onto his back to seemingly find a more comfortable position. I am trying my best to reach his head as I am now straddled across his stomach with my tiny legs stretched on the outside of his waist. Uncle Charlie's body moved slowly in a circular motion, rolling, to what I now know as an adult is known as grinding and gyrating. I felt petrified and scared to move as his hand clutched the item Mommy termed "a ding -a -ling;" the thing that only little boys have and that a little girl should never see or touch. I had no idea what to do. I had no idea what was going on. He jerked himself faster and harder, holding my hip with one hand and his penis with the other; now stomach to stomach, my face to his chest. Until last, the volcano erupted; ejaculation from masturbation rested on my lower back, inches from my buttocks! Uncle Charlie now sends me back into the living room, bewildered and abused.

I was perplexed as to what had just occurred. Now I'm standing in the center of the kitchen floor, close to my grandma, thinking what would happen now that I told her this story? Following a few seconds of stillness and hesitation, my grandma then summons my Aunt Sue. "Sue, please come here." When Sue enters the room, she adds, "Take LaTonya and give her a bath, and make sure you thoroughly wash her hands." It was almost as if she wanted to make certain there was no trace of my uncle's presence and just wash away the evidence. Sue fulfilled my grandmother's request. Our granny, you see, did not play (a word used metaphorically to mean taking all things seriously, what she said, she meant). Because her bark and bite were equally ferocious, when she screamed "move," everyone moved!

I sat in a small tub of water with a washcloth in my hand, wondering, "so, that's it?" as I shivered and felt tiny goosebumps form on my chest and arms thinking what in the heck just occurred? Here I am, a preschooler, once innocent, but the spirit of abuse has altered the course of my upbringing in what seems like only minutes. It was then that I realized something had abruptly shifted, but I couldn't put my finger on what it was. Even as a young child, I knew I wanted answers, whether they came in the shape of a simple explanation or a more complex survival manual.

In Ephesians 6:12, the Bible says that "for we wrestle not against flesh and blood, but against principalities, spiritual wickedness in high places." Yes, I know how my adversary thinks and acts. He's a master manipulator and mastermind. He used my Uncle Charlie, my grandmother, my Uncle Steven, and my Aunt Sue to launch his first attack against me when I was a little girl on my way to greatness and purpose. LaTonya, only five years old, was forced to fend for herself against giants and the devil (Ephesians 6:11). Those who were supposed to look out for me — the babysitters, the relatives — let the enemy's spirit use their body as a vessel to gain access to me and assault me. This was the first step on a path that would lead to similar situations in the future.

In this book, I will take you through the chronological voyage of my life, including its highs and lows, its ups and downs, and its rollercoaster ride. I will share how God saved and delivered me, even during times when I felt like giving up. I will also share how I learned to understand my purpose and the person God created me to be. My goal as an imperfect example of Christ, is to empower others through my stories, encouragement, and love. My hope is that this book, which is also God's book, will bring you freedom, power, and renewed hope as you discover your own purpose and help others do the same.

CHAPTER 1

What Just Happened

I was born in 1971 as the eldest fourth-generation child to George and Debra. As an only child, I was loved by both my parents' families. My parents met in Orange Grove Projects, where my dad, a ladies' man, swept my mom off her feet with his dark skin, good looks, and white teeth. My mom, a quiet, subtle southern belle, captivated my dad with her beauty and majorette legs. Despite their strong chemistry, their relationship didn't last long beyond my mother's pregnancy with me.

Growing up, I was surrounded by loving grandparents, aunts, and uncles who took great care of me. For a few years, I was the only child on both my mom's and dad's side, so I always had the attention I needed. As I grew older, my teenage aunts and uncles became my playmates, babysitters, and mentors, and I learned by modeling their behaviors.

Latonya M. Whitehead

My uncle Johnny was particularly special to me. He was the youngest of all my uncles, and only a few years older than me. We spent most of my childhood years together as playmates. He taught me how to be a tom-boy, how to climb trees and pick berries along the railroad tracks and bushes. He even taught me how to play flag football and jump fences. I still have a scar on my left knee from when I tried to jump a chain-link fence and didn't quite make it.

Johnny was like the older brother I never had. I remember one time when a boy was bullying me on my school bus. The bus stop was right in front of Johnny's house, and when he heard about what was happening, he got on the bus and defended me, causing the boy to have a seizure. While the seizure is not something to brag about, it is a reminder of how my uncle always had my back and protected me.

I remember once my mom got three tickets to the circus and asked me to choose a friend to come with us. I chose Johnny, who I like to think of as my brother, but my mom had several objections to him going. She wanted me to choose someone who fit her vision of what a proper circus companion should be, someone who was prim, proper and dainty. However, I saw Johnny as my closest friend at that time, and I didn't understand why he couldn't come with us.

My mother's preference to always impress the Jones' made her fear bad thoughts and judgments from others, which made her self-conscious about her decisions. She tried to find excuses why Johnny wasn't the right candidate for the circus trip. One reason was that he was a boy, another was that he wouldn't have the right clothes to wear and finally, she said he was just "bad." But I knew that my brother was perfect to me and I couldn't understand why my mom couldn't see that.

Despite my mother's objections, I stood my ground and made it clear that if Johnny wasn't going to the circus, neither was I. Although my mother was angry, she eventually allowed me to have my way. This experience taught me the importance of standing up for what I believe in and valuing the people in my life, even if they may not fit society's conventional mold of what is considered acceptable.

It was our first time at a circus and we were in awe of the grandeur of the place. The bright lights, the elephants, lions, and all the other animals and people made it a truly captivating experience. Johnny and I were both amazed, as we had never seen anything like it before.

However, things took a turn when Johnny, being the adventurous one, decided to take a solo tour of the circus. This sent my mom into a rage. I couldn't help but focus on Johnny and his boldness, rather than the circus performances. I wanted to join him and take a risk too, but the look on my mom's face made it clear that this would not be a good idea.

After the circus, we headed home, which was only a two-minute drive from my grandma's where my mom and I lived. The drive was eerily quiet, and it felt as though an elephant from the circus had joined us. Once we got home, my mom unleashed her fury on me. She was so angry that she said "This was your last circus and Johnny would never go anywhere with us again!" I tried to speak up in my defense, but she wouldn't listen. I took the blame for my brother, and that was the last circus I ever saw.

Going back to my childhood, I have fond memories of learning new things and discovering the world around me. One such memory is of the day I found a balloon in the yard while playing. I was determined to blow it up by mouth, but it wouldn't inflate. So, I ran inside to fill it with water to check for any holes. As I was exiting the bathroom, my uncle Johnny asked me, "what are you doing?" I began to explain my failed attempts at blowing up the balloon. To my surprise, Johnny, my uncle Wesley, Aunt Brenda and Uncle Reg, burst into uncontrollable laughter.

Their laughter was so intense that it became contagious, and soon I was laughing too, even though I had no idea why. Have you ever experienced something like this, where someone's laughter is so contagious that it makes you laugh for no reason at all? That's exactly what happened to me that day.

After we settled down, wiping away tears of laughter, my uncle Johnny explained to me that the thin, see-through, narrow balloon was called a rubber (condom) and that no matter how hard I blew, it would never inflate to my expectations. He then went on to explain the concept of condoms and the "birds and the bees" to me. This was the day I learned about the facts of life and the importance of safe sex.

In spite of my privilege as an only child, only niece, and only grandchild, it took me a long time to break free from some abuse in my family. I learnt early on that keeping quiet was for the best, as there were more likely secrets about the occasional defilements that took place. Do you remember the sexual abuse I faced when I was five? Even at the age of eleven, their true colors were beginning to appear, still using those I loved to hurt me.

I recall vividly going to the beach with my aunts and uncles, terrified of the deep but yet shallow water at Fairhope Pier, when one of my uncles decided to take away my fear factor by leading me out to the somewhat deeper end of the water. He takes me up from the water and literally dumps me back in, akin to a body slam wrestling maneuver, after celebrating the vanquished fear with me. Being slender my entire life and weighing around eighty pounds in sixth grade, dropping me in that water was a simple task for him and, understandably, terrifying for me. Because I was unprepared, this slam drove my entire body to dive under water; even with my eyes wide open, I could not see the attack coming! This is an illustration of how the enemy operates. Even with your eyes wide open, you can be taken by surprise or caught off guard. In the book of Genesis, Chapter 3, the serpent approached Eve as a friend and a helper. However, He failed to mention there would be downfall and introduction to death when she submitted to his tactic. Genesis chapter 2:15-16 states, *"The LORD God, took the man and put him in the Garden of Eden to work and take care of "it. And the LORD God commanded the man, "You are free to eat from any tree in the garden; but you must not from the tree of the knowledge of good and evil, for when you eat from it you will certainly die."* My uncle, in a spiritual form of a serpent, had forgotten to warn me of the dangers that lie ahead while going into the deeps of the water. He had forgotten to mention, the manipulation. He forgot to mention the possibility of my spiritual death.

After making a massive lunge under the water, he rapidly grabs me out of the water in an act of "rescuing the little damsel in distress," all the while sticking his hand down my bikini bottom and poking my vagina with his finger. "Really!" Honestly, I couldn't believe it! My uncle dried off with a towel on the beach after emerging from the sea, and he laughed as if nothing had occurred. In the midst of my confusion, I kept wondering, "What the heck just happened, and why?" Another uncle has just groped me here.

Reflecting back on my childhood, I realize that the enemy had a specific plan to target me through sexual abuse and molestation. This traumatic experience not only introduced me to the topic of sex in a negative manner, but it also greatly impacted my self-esteem. The abuse and molestation caused me to have low self-esteem, self-doubt, insecurity, and self-inflicted wounds. These negative feelings and experiences attempted to prevent me from reaching my full potential and achieving my goals. The enemy hoped that by causing these emotional and psychological wounds, it would ultimately lead to my downfall and prevent me from achieving my purpose in life. "But God!" John 10: 10 *"The thief comes only to steal, and to kill and to destroy; I came that they would have life, and might have it more abundantly."* We tend to think the only job of the thief is to take something. Clearly, in John 10:10 we understand his mission and his goal is more than that. He wants to kill, steal and destroy. "But God…" sending his only son so that you and I can live. But wait! There's more! God doesn't just want us to live but live a life of abundance. Trust me, I understand from first-hand experience how the thief can take from you, leaving you hurt, empty, broken, and even discouraged. I understand what it feels like to be molested into silence, having the type of hurt that makes you wish you were dead, had killed yourself, or that someone would've just killed you instead. The type of pain that will have you forty – years later writing a book about it, shining a light on all those nasty areas of darkness, removing your band-aid, peeling off the scabs to your wounds, showing your bloody scars in order to help heal someone else. This life has not certainly been easy, but with God, we can make it; by first seeing hope, trusting it's process, and saying, "Lord, I graciously accept your challenge." My hope with the exposure of my life traumas rises, and falls is that my story of redemption, grace, and mercy will help you that's reading, and in return, you will help someone else; as only God will get the Glory from our stories.

CHAPTER 2

Speak Up, Say Something

The transition from Crichton Elementary to Booker Washington Middle School was a significant one for me. At Crichton, I was the favorite of my fifth-grade teacher, Mrs. McDonald. I was a straight-A student, I was given special tasks such as running errands for my teacher and taking names of class interrupters in her absence, and I was even chosen to be the traffic guard and hall monitor without ever having signed up for it. However, my experience at Booker Washington was vastly different. I found myself feeling out of place and struggling to adjust to the new environment. The principal, Mr. Marshall, was strict and demanding, but also fair in his expectations. He expected and received respect from all students and enforced strict rules such as walking on the correct side of the halls and remaining silent when he entered the room. He knew the names of both the disruptive students and the academically successful ones. I often wished

I stood out as a student of valor, bravery, and intelligence, so that Mr. Marshall would have recognized my name and spoken to me personally as I walked the halls.

At Booker T. Washington Middle School, I felt invisible and insignificant. Many of the girls at the school were more physically developed than I was, with curvaceous bodies that were considered attractive and desirable. In contrast, I felt plain and unremarkable. When I looked in a mirror, I was ugly. The kind of ugly Shug Avery calls Sealy in the movie, The Color Purple. I was skinny, with a small head and large eyeglasses that didn't suit my narrow face. My teeth were crooked, my gums were too big for my mouth, and my hair was thin and damaged from overuse of Saturday morning pressing combs.

One of the most difficult experiences for me at the school was Physical Education class. The other girls would come into the locker room wearing bras and even thongs, while I was self-conscious about my flat chest and lack of development. I would try to hide my body by turning my back, but I was still teased and made fun of for my small size and lack of curves. The bullying extended to my clothing as well, with other students teasing me for wearing knock-off penny loafers and tennis shoes. Overall, it was a tough and embarrassing way to start my middle school journey.

There were so many students at Booker T. Washington Middle School with different personalities and backgrounds. The school was predominantly black, with many students coming from the Toulminville area, specifically the Roger Williams housing complex. Being from Orange Grove, I was aware that there was a rivalry between the two communities, with each being taught to avoid the other. This made it difficult for me to navigate my new environment and figure out where I fit in.

In the seventh grade, I decided to take control of my own identity and try to become someone of importance. I decided to join the track and field team, inspired by my uncle Alonzo who had been a successful runner in high school. Despite never having run track before, I made the team and was placed on the sprint team, competing in the quarter, one- and two-hundred-yard dashes, and my favorite, the four by one-hundred-meter relay. I performed well, often placing within the top three in my heats and our team was even winning some meets. This experience gave me more confidence, even though I didn't have support from my family during my races.

As I was part of the volleyball team, I had high hopes for my performance. I had made the team and had never missed a practice, working hard to improve and earn a chance to play in games. However, my coach, Miss Vicks, hardly gave me any opportunities to play. This was a difficult and frustrating experience for me, as I felt that my hard work and dedication was not being recognized. I wished that I had the courage and confidence to speak up and respectfully ask my coach why I was being excluded. This was one of the many moments where I longed for the support and guidance of my parents or extended family members. If my performance was the issue, I hoped that my coach would have helped me to improve and become a better player. However, I didn't know how to communicate my feelings and concerns effectively. This neglect, coupled with all the struggles and insecurities I had faced in the past, left me feeling like a failure.

Meanwhile, a significant change was happening in my personal life. My grandmother, whom I called Granny, moved to 121 N. Carlen Street, still within the district for my school, Booker T. Washington. This meant that my mother would take me to school in the mornings and I would walk home alone to Granny's in the evenings. The two-mile stretch home was filled with fear, but eventually, I met a girl named Tisa who lived on Margaret Street, just one block away from Granny's. We met while I was walking home from school one day, and it was the beginning of a new friendship that helped me navigate through the struggles I was facing.

As I entered the seventh grade, I found myself searching for answers about who I was, what I wanted to become, and how to fit in among the many different and conflicting personalities at my all-black school, Booker T. Washington. Despite the challenges I faced, I discovered a new friend in Tisa. We bonded over our shared experiences and interests, including dancing, singing, and experimenting with makeup. We even went as far as sneaking a change of clothes in our backpacks and wearing lipstick and eyeliner when we were out of sight of our parents.

Despite our close friendship, Tisa and I were not among the most elite or popular students at school. We both struggled with feelings of low self-esteem, but for different reasons. I felt out of place because of the bullying I had experienced in the past, while Tisa was taller than the average seventh grader. She was a shotput thrower on the track and field team, and I couldn't help but envy her physical strength and size.

Despite our differences, Tisa and I were each other's only friends, and we had a close bond as best friends. We were each other's support system during a time when we felt like outsiders and didn't quite fit in. It was through this friendship that I began to gain more confidence in myself and my abilities.

As the ringleader of our mischief, I convinced my best friend Tisa to secretly host a small house party on National Skip-Day. For those unfamiliar, National Skip-Day is a day set aside for senior high school students to skip school and do something fun. Many students go to the beach, have parties, or do other activities. Tisa and I decided to throw a party at her house while her parents were at work. We invited all the popular boys and even managed to get a hold of a bottle of Mad Dog 2020, a cheap wine in the Orange Jubilee flavor. Despite having no experience or knowledge of alcohol, we insisted on drinking it. The party was a huge success and Tisa and I felt like we were on top of the world with the popular boys paying attention to us.

As the party went on, I whispered to Tisa "Should I tell him?" Tisa replied, "Tell who what?" I replied, "Should I tell Shay? Should I tell him I have a secret crush on him?" Shay was the cutest boy in school, with light skin, freckles, pink lips, a beautiful smile, and mesmerizing green eyes that sometimes looked gray. I had a huge crush on him, but I had only confided in Tisa about it.

Well instead of me approaching Shay, because I had no voice and too afraid to talk, Tisa being much bolder than I, delivered the message for me. Shay then responds with a message for me to meet him in the bedroom to talk. While sitting on the bed, Shay questions my love for him. What is love to a seventh grader, I wonder? Is it the tingly butterfly feeling I got in my stomach, the racing heartbeat, or the blush I tried to contain whenever I saw him? Our chat was frequently interrupted by the other childish boys bursting into the room from time to time as I began to explain that I had liked and observed him since sixth grade. Shay and I start kissing in a quiet moment. I had never before kissed a boy. He gently inserted his tongue into my mouth, and I reciprocated. We kissed passionately with our tongues for what seemed like hours. I'm not sure whether I did it correctly, but it sure felt amazing. It was like something out of a movie. The kiss was slow, and then he began to touch me gently. This was not only my first kiss, but also my first contact from a male who was not related to me. Shay starts rubbing my body in private places. I cringed, innocently, and tightened my legs shut. I asked Shay to stop. "If you love me, you would let me do it!" he said while he continued. Because I adored Shay, I allowed him to

17

continuously touch me in awkward places and kiss me inappropriately. Shay then starts unzipping his pants while still kissing me and attempting to take my pants down while pulling out his penis. I begin to tell him to "stop!" because I am terrified. "Stop Shay!" I exclaimed repeatedly. "Please stop!" "Come on, Shay stop!" His body pressed against me as he tried to pull my pants down, and I struggled to pull them back up with one hand because my other hand was trapped between the wall and Tisa's bed. I'm trying to clench my legs closed with my pants halfway down when the four boys rush back into the room.

On a mission, the boys set out to aid Shay, their action took a cruel turn, as they forced my arm down and spread my legs wide. Shay finally gets a few hard blows into my vagina. Immediately, my best friend, like a hero in a Marvel movie, charged in and fought to break their siege. She threw the boys off with all her might, and saved me from further assault.

I couldn't believe that my middle school secret crush raped me in Tisa's bed. I was heartbroken and ashamed! How does this cycle continue to find me? Why am I always manipulated, molested, and defeated? Why do my horrific life stories keep me silent?

After a few days of school, my best friend Tisa distanced herself from me for fear of getting in trouble after the rumors began to circulate. The story was that I let the boys run a train on me. The Urban Dictionary defines a train as consensual sexual interaction between one female and two or more males waiting in line to have it. My classmates didn't know I was raped by five popular boys. All the girls wanted these boys — they were handsome, athletic, and wore designer clothes and shoes. They raped me! Four participated, and one was a predator who used my adolescent love to get what he wanted. I was raped in seventh grade and was too afraid to tell anyone!

In the book of Exodus, God provided Moses with specific instructions on how to fulfill his mission of leading the Israelites out of Egypt. Moses, feeling overwhelmed by the task, initially protested to God by citing his speech impediment as the reason he couldn't lead. The Bible does not specify the exact nature of Moses' speech problem, but it could have been a stutter, a fear of public speaking (glossophobia), or a slow speaking pace. However, God reminds us through the scripture, "For God has not given us a spirit of fear, but of power and of love and of a sound mind" (2 Timothy 1:7). This passage reminds us that fear does not come from God, and we should not be afraid to share our testimonies and speak up about the things that have wronged us. With prayer and guidance from God, we can overcome our fears and speak confidently.

The purpose of my life and yours requires sacrifice. My calling has required me to reveal personal and often difficult aspects of my life, such as naming those who have harmed me, exposing predators, and giving glory to the one true God who has set me free. In this book, I share experiences that are humbling and embarrassing. As I wrote, I wondered how readers would perceive me, and if my family would still accept me. However, this book is not about me. It's about obedience and honor. Obedience means pushing past fears and insecurities, even when it feels uncomfortable. For years, I made excuses and tried to avoid this part of my purpose, just like Moses did. I told God I couldn't write, I didn't have the qualifications, and I barely graduated high school. But God continued to tell me to "Finish the book!" My obedience to God is not about achieving a specific outcome, it's about showing honor to Him. I do what He says because I honor who He is.

Our past and salvation is not about us, but about the love and grace of God, who sent his son to save us. Every testimony begins with a test, and as I write, I gain strength from each word. It is essential to speak up and speak out about experiences of molestation, rape, abuse, and neglect. Keeping silent about these traumatic events only prolongs the healing process. I want to let you know that you are not alone in your experiences. Forgiveness, expression, and speaking out are key to healing and freeing ourselves and others from the shackles of these traumatic events. Don't be afraid to use your voice and share your story. Someone is waiting to hear it and it may also help them to heal.

CHAPTER 3

The Big Cat-Fish

You should have a good idea of the many challenges I've faced at such a young age by now. Trust me, this is not an attempt to play the victim, despite the fact that I was victimized; rather, my goal is for you to capture my nakedness, transparency, and ability to overcome with God's help. Life, as I saw it as a little girl growing into my preteens, never loved me. A lonely little girl was always looking for validation and attention. I was left vulnerable because I was seeking such stability. As my life story unfolds, I often say, "I am every woman," referring to Whitney Houston's song. I don't think there are any obstacles I haven't overcome, including the humiliation of being cat-fished.

Still in eighth grade at Washington Middle School. I later met a new friend; we became friends because we shared the same middle and last name, as well as playing clarinet in the band and taking many of the same classes. We were the Laverne and Shirley of our generation. With a little more assurance now, I finally had a friend who shared some of my interests; until the plot thickens.

My friend, Natalie, and I were incredibly close. We shared intimate stories about our families and growing up, even discussing some of the difficult experiences we had faced. But one day, everything changed. Natalie called me with a surprise: she had a male cousin she wanted me to meet.

As a young girl, I had been told by my mother that I shouldn't date or talk to boys on the phone. So, in order to keep our conversations secret, Natalie devised a plan. She would call me on a three-way call with her cousin, Michael, on the other end. We would talk for hours, with Natalie sitting quietly on the line, ready to jump in and make it sound like we were just a group of girls talking if my mother happened to pick up the other end of the phone.

Looking back, I'm not sure why we went to such lengths to hide our conversations. Michael's voice hadn't yet reached the level of maturity, and he sounded just like one of the girls. But at the time, it seemed like the only way to maintain our secret friendship.

Boyfriend and girlfriend through the telephone for months without ever seeing each other's faces, *"Michael and Tonya sitting in a tree K.I.S.S.I.N.G, first comes love then comes marriage, then comes Tonya with a baby carriage."* This was our theme song. You know, this took place in the late eighty's where there were no cellular phones, or facetime capabilities. Every morning before school, and every evening after school,

Michael and I would talk on the landline, creeping secretly by telephone, displaying our love for each other.

At this moment in my life, I am feeling incredibly confident and self-assured. I have a new group of friends and a secret older boyfriend that my mother knows nothing about. His name is Michael and he is a junior at Williamson High School, while I am in the eighth grade. We became inseparable over the phone, talking for hours on end. However, I am not sure what I did to get in trouble, but my punishment was severe. My mother took away my phone privileges. This left me feeling lost and unsure of what to do next.

Do you remember the long walk home from school that I used to take in the sixth and seventh grades? Although my mother and I had moved to Chateau Oaks Apartments, my grandmother never left Carlen Street. So, I continued to take that long walk home, but now with a sense of longing for Michael. Usually, when I reached my grandmother's house, no one was home, so I had the opportunity to talk to Michael as much as I wanted until someone came home. In addition, we started sending letters to each other through the mail, which was how we finally got to see each other, by sending pictures taken with a polaroid camera.

Our relationship had been going strong throughout my eighth-grade year in middle school and was now heading into the summer of my ninth-grade year. We still had our regular phone calls and romantic phone conversations. However, things changed when my aunt moved to Montgomery Street in Prichard, which was just a few miles away from Michael's house. This presented an opportunity for Michael and I to come up with a plan. I would sleepover at my aunt's house and ask her if Michael could come over for a visit.

My aunt was one of my favorite relatives and we had a great relationship. She was down-to-earth and we could talk about anything. I also knew she was curious about seeing what Michael looked like. So, on a Saturday, Michael was going to come over for a visit. He called me when he was on his way, but he had to walk because he didn't have a car. I was waiting anxiously for him to arrive, running back and forth, peeking through the living room curtains to see if he was walking up the driveway. But when he finally arrived, he was standing under a tree across the street. I could see him from the window, but he wouldn't come over. I could see that he had a light-skinned complexion, an Afro-Jerry curl, and he was wearing navy blue Levi jeans, a white pullover sweatshirt, and red high-top Converse. He looked cute from a distance, but I couldn't understand why he was being so distant.

My uncle emerged from the house and stepped onto the porch, lighting a cigarette as he did so often. "Why is he over there?" he asked, gesturing towards a figure in the distance. I shrugged, unsure of the answer. My uncle was a formidable presence - standing at a towering six feet four inches and weighing in at 290 pounds of intimidating muscle. Despite my uncle's calls for him to come over, the figure simply walked away, heading towards his home.

Confused and unsure of what had just happened, I watched him go. Had I not lived up to the polaroid expectation? Was it something I had said or done?

It wasn't until later that evening when Michael called to explain his sudden departure. "I was afraid of your uncle," he confessed. And there it was - my chance to meet my first true love, diminished by fear. Though our first encounter had been cut short, I knew that opportunities would present themselves again in the future.

As I entered the ninth grade at Murphy High School, I struggled to find my place among my peers. Despite this, my romance with Michael continued to flourish through our secret rendezvous during school hours. Our master plan was simple: my step-father would drop me off at the rear of the school, where I would then skip class and walk two miles to a park on Emogene Street where Michael would be waiting for me.

We spent our days in the park, talking and making goo-goo eyes, eating chips and candy, and sharing blushes and smiles until it was time for school to dismiss. Then, Michael would catch the city bus and I would walk back to school just in time for track practice. This became our routine at least three times a week, each meeting becoming more passionate than the last. We were in love, and our education and attendance at school seemed of little importance to us.

But as the first quarter came to an end and report cards were distributed, our secret love was put to the test. My report card showed that I had missed 21 days of school, an oversight that I had tried to cover up by altering the document with liquid paper. But my parents were not fooled, and I was punished severely - confined to my room, with no telephone or outdoor privileges, allowed out only to eat and use the bathroom. This punishment, of course, put a strain on my relationship with Michael, and I feared he would leave me for someone at his own school.

As I served my punishment, at my Granny's house, I continued to talk to Michael, my secret lover. We were still in love and planning to marry as soon as I graduated in three years. However, one hot summer night, I grew tired of the punishment and decided to run away from home. My plan was to live with Michael and his mother. I left my parents' house on Acacia Street in Crichton in the middle of the night and walked up Moffat Road in the hopes of getting a ride to my Romeo or having him come to rescue me.

After finally making it to a gas station, I used the coins from my piggy bank to call Michael from the payphone. I told him my whereabouts and my plan to relocate with him and his mother. Michael was angry and tried to calm me, assuring me that someone was coming to pick me up. However, I waited anxiously and no one came.

As I leaned against the phone booth, feeling both anxious and sleepy, I saw a car turning into the gas station that looked very familiar. It was a 1979 burgundy Pontiac Grand Prix, shiny and well-maintained like it had just come from the showroom floor. It was my Uncle Carl's car, and I recognized it immediately. He walked past me, giving me a nod, and went into the gas station. I was on the phone with Michael telling him, "You won't believe who just pulled up," and he replied, "It's your uncle. I called him to pick you up." I was in disbelief and even more angry that my "knight in shining armor" did not come to rescue me from the smells of gasoline and the oil-spilled pavement of this mom-and-pop convenience store.

My Uncle Carl headed out of the store and simply said to me, "let's go." I hung up the payphone and got in the car, where my uncle and I exchanged no words. I thought he would be taking me to my mom, but instead, I went home with him and my aunt. After I got there, Michael and I talked on the phone until we both drifted into sleep.

The morning after my impulsive decision to run away, my mother arrived to take me home. However, her intentions were not what I had expected. The night I had left, she had called the police and shared the letters that Michael and I had been writing to each other. She even went as far as to send the police to his house, using the address she found on the postal envelopes. Her hope was that they would find me there. All of this had taken place while I was on my long walk to the gas station.

As I sat in the car with my mother, I braced myself for the punishment that I knew was coming. However, instead of heading home, she made a detour to Toulminville and had me admitted to the youth center as a runaway. I was devastated, angry, and felt betrayed by my own mother. I was now in the Crisis Center of the Mobile County Youth Center, unsure of how long I would be there but it felt like months. I had no communication with my family, friends, or the love of my life.

Over the years, I had learned to be cunning and manipulative. The staff at the youth center took a liking to me. They found me to be respectful, and couldn't understand why such a sweet little girl like me was there. I used their affection to my advantage, convincing two of the staff members to let me use the phone to call my father and Michael. However, neither of them answered my calls that day.

God has a funny way of healing. He often places us in situations where we are isolated and separated from everything and everyone we think we need in order to survive. Like Jonah in the Bible, many of us have our own plans and timelines for our lives, but we pay a penalty for not following God's plan. Jonah wanted to go to Tarshish, but God's clear instruction was for him to go to Nineveh and preach the gospel. Despite this, Jonah chose to do things his own way and fled the presence of God. However, as Jonah soon found out, it is impossible to flee from an omnipresent God. On his journey to Tarshish, God caused turmoil on the ship, putting everyone in danger and ultimately leading to Jonah being thrown off the boat and into the belly of a big fish. In this isolated and dire situation, Jonah called out to the Lord.

As I sat in the youth center, feeling distressed and hopeless, I came to realize the true weight of my disobedience. Admitting my wrongs was a difficult and painful process, but it was necessary for my spiritual growth. I found myself in the depths of despair, feeling as though I was trapped in the belly of a great fish, with God as my only way out. The depression that had begun to consume me felt overwhelming, and I feared that if God didn't intervene, I would be lost forever.

Even as a teenager, I knew that I didn't like the person I was becoming. I was uncomfortable with who I was and the actions I had taken. I began to take responsibility for my failures, instead of placing blame on others for my "demonic actions." I knew that the Lord was dealing with me, and I was determined to change my ways.

When my time was up, one Monday, my mother was there to pick me up. After I was released, she began asking difficult questions about Michael and me in the car. "Had we ever had intercourse?" "Did I know his real name?" "Has he ever sexually forced himself on me?" she inquired. I was befuddled once more until we arrived at the youth detective station. There, I was introduced to a female detective who began asking similar questions to my mother before revealing Michael Williams' real name was Shannon. "Michael was a girl who had pretended to be a boy for the past two years," she explained. "Michael was denying me and our relationship!" she added. She went on to say that Michael and I would be meeting in a matter of minutes.

As the detective led us to a larger room, we sat in silence, awaiting the arrival of Michael and his mother. To our surprise, the first person to enter the room was not Michael, but a young woman, formerly known as Michael. She was dressed in black Levi denims, jingling baby earrings, fire red lipstick, and red pumps. My mind raced as I struggled to process this revelation.

"You've got to be kidding me," I exclaimed. "Michael is a girl for real?" My confusion quickly turned to anger as I remembered all of the lies and deceit that Michael had inflicted upon me. As I sat there, watching her deny ever knowing me, I knew that I could no longer remain silent.

With determination in my voice, I stood up for myself, telling the truth about my past experiences with Michael. I refused to be left ridiculed and mocked, and I would not allow the enemy to force me into silence once again. My closing statements sealed the deal, and finally, Michael (now known as Shannon) admitted her dishonesty and frailties.

The experience was a harsh but a valuable lesson. Just a few days prior, I had found myself spiritually isolated in the belly of a big fish, much like Jonah in the Bible. It was not until I chose to trust God and do His will that He delivered me. In 2 Corinthians 12:9, God reminds us that His grace is all we need and that His power is made perfect in our weakness. It was only when I became weak that God was able to show Himself strong.

From that day forward, I never spoke to Shannon again. I had gone from the spiritual belly of a big fish to being awakened by a cat-fish. But through it all, I learned that the key to healing is simple, yet not easy: trust God. Talk to Him, and He will listen. Ask Him, and He will answer. In the end, His grace through His son Jesus Christ is all we ever need to survive.

CHAPTER 4

Baby on Board

Writing this chapter is incredibly difficult for me. There are many wounds that I must open in order to tell this story, and I do not want to hurt or embarrass those I love by reliving this period of our past. This chapter takes place between 1988 and 1991, a time when my father and stepmother were facing challenges in their marriage, and my mother and stepfather were going through a difficult separation. In the midst of all of this, my father and mother were also locked in a bitter custody battle over me, which ultimately resulted in my father gaining every other weekend visit, every other major holiday visit, and one month in the summer, while also paying child support.

These were critical years for me, as I was in high school and had to witness the fights and arguments happening in both households until their eventual divorce. The only happy memories I have from this time are when my stepmother and

I would spend all day at the mall on any given Saturday, shopping for Christmas in July. She was a master at finding great deals, and she always made sure to buy gifts for everyone early. The other happy memories I have are when my stepfather, L.P. and I would be in our den in the Cottagehill Road townhouse. I would watch him play his instruments as he prepared for his next band gig, and he would often pass me the microphone, telling me I could really sing. On Thursday nights, he and I would watch our weekly television lineup, which included The Wheel of Fortune, The Cosby Show, and A Different World. All the other nights, he had band practice and gigs to play on the weekends.

My mother during this period had graduated from nursing school and began working as an RN at Mobile Infirmary Hospital, and our mother-daughter time was greatly depleted. She worked the 2 PM to 10 PM shift, and by the time she came home, I was already asleep or in bed. But I remember those moments when she would sneak into my room for a goodnight sayonara or nightcap. I would pretend to be asleep, feigning the deep breaths of slumber as I watched the peeking of the hall light and her shadow on my wall. I did this because it's what all the kids on television did when their parents entered their rooms. Despite this, I felt that I never had any real affection or connection with my mother, and I longed for it.

Please keep an open mind and heart as I share this story of the struggles and growing pains that my mother and I have overcome and embraced. We may have had our difficulties, but we are now a reflection of God's image of a mother-daughter relationship. Our story is one of guilt, fault, and forgiveness. But, it's important to remember that as we seek the Father in prayer, we must not hold anything against anyone and forgive, as stated in Mark 11:25, "And when you stand praying, if you hold anything against anyone, forgive them, so that your Father in heaven may forgive your sins." My mother and I have long since moved past these issues, and we have forgiven each other, ourselves, and have been forgiven. It's important to remember that none of us are perfect, not me as a daughter, or my parents as parents. We are all equally flawed, and I hope that this story will inspire understanding and empathy, rather than judgment.

As I entered my senior year of high school, I was still struggling with deception and dishonesty. My lips were so full of lies that there was no truth to be found in them. It was during this time that I met my son's father on a Greyhound bus while traveling to visit my aunt Freda and uncle Carl in North Carolina. The summer of 1989 was a turning point in my life, as it was the first time, I had seen my aunt and uncle since they had moved away a few years prior. My son's father, a native of Sylacauga, Alabama, was also on the bus, in route to visit his aunt in Virginia for the summer. We exchanged numbers and continued to talk throughout the summer, even after we both returned home. He would often make the drive to Mobile to visit me on the weekends.

However, my behavior at the time was far from exemplary. I was still lying and being deceptive, using my parents' lack of monitoring as an opportunity to forge permission slips for track to sneak away for weekend visits. This continued until January of 1989, when I found out I was pregnant with my son Jarred.

When my mother found out, she was furious and refused to accept her role as a grandmother. In a desperate attempt to protect my future, she even took me to a friend of hers that was a doctor to discuss the possibility of an abortion. It was only in this moment that my future became important to her, despite the fact that we had never discussed college or career plans before.

Despite the challenges and mistakes of my past, I have come to understand and accept that we are all imperfect and that forgiveness is key in moving forward. My relationship with my mother and son's father may have been fraught with struggles, but through forgiveness and understanding, we have been able to overcome and build a stronger bond.

As I sat in the doctor's office, I knew there was only one thing I could say in response to the suggestion that I terminate my pregnancy: "I am not killing my baby." This final statement marked the beginning of a tumultuous journey for me.

Upon returning home to the Carondelet Court Apartments, where my mother and I now lived following her divorce from my stepfather, I was met with a barrage of angry words from my mother. She berated me for embarrassing her in front of her doctor friend, for refusing to be a grandmother, and for the "straw that broke the camel's back" - her ultimatum that if I chose to have the baby, I would have to leave her home.

The argument between my mother and I escalated into a physical altercation, and I know that in the black culture, hitting your mother is a grave offense and similar to committing suicide but before you pass judgment, please hear the rest of my story.

Though I knew I shouldn't have hit my mother, I didn't die that night. However, the police were called, and I soon found myself leaving my mother's house to live with father and his wife, Neicy, for a short period of time. This living arrangement, though it granted me more freedom, was unhealthy and dysfunctional. My father had become abusive towards Neicy, and their marriage was on the brink of collapse.

I watched as my father's addiction to cocaine consumed him, as he left the house day after day, taking pieces of the home with him and never returning them. Neicy eventually left for her own apartment, leaving me to care for my younger brother and sister, DJ and Shantai, until she was able to get back on her feet.

Despite the turmoil and dysfunction, Neicy took me and my unborn child in and gave us a sense of stability and security although she didn't have to. She eventually separated from my father, and began her self-healing.

Rewinding back to the day I first met my stepmother, Neicy, on Davidson Street. She was my father's new girlfriend and from that day on, our relationship has been unbreakable. Even after forty years, our love for each other remains unconditional.

During the time I was pregnant and finishing my senior year in high school, Neicy helped me to obtain my first job at Shoe City on Government Street. As I think back on those days, I can't help but smile, even though they were difficult times. I often wonder how I was able to find joy in such dark places.

As the birth of my son approached, my relationship with my mother began to improve. We needed to repair the broken bond between us. On September 26, 1990, I gave birth to my son, but instead of returning to Neicy's, I decided to work on rebuilding my relationship with my mother. It was a challenging time for both of us, as we were both emotionally struggling and did not know how to communicate effectively with one another. We both needed healing.

When I returned to my mother's, she had decorated my bedroom and placed a crib in the room for my son. She had also bought him a baby mobile that served as a night light on the wall. My mother was trying her best, but our relationship still had its challenges. Despite this, I knew that my time at her home would not be permanent.

My mother had my baby brother, TJ, who was three years older than my son at this time. I understand why she wasn't ready to be a grandmother prematurely, but we couldn't change what had already happened. She was afraid, uncertain, and lost at that time, as a divorced and single parent once again. It had been sixteen years since she had her second baby and now, she had to deal with the thought of caring for my son and me too.

I was unemployed, fresh out of high school, and living with my single mother and younger brother. My mother, a traveling nurse, was working in New Orleans, and I was able to live rent-free with her in exchange for helping with childcare for my brother, TJ. Everything was going smoothly, until one day, I was caught in a compromising situation with a boy in the house. My mother, following the age-old adage "when you think you're grown, you've got to get out of my house," kicked me out.

I was in a state of rebellion and adversity had become my greatest enemy. I was reaping what I had sown, and I didn't deserve to be absolved of my sins. But just like the woman in Luke 7, I recognized who Jesus was and humbled myself. I washed His feet with my tears, not caring about the judgment of others or the rumors circulating about me. All I cared about was being transformed.

The bottom line is, change requires humility and a willingness to stretch oneself. If you seek the Father, He will meet you where you are. But it's important not to allow sin to consume you to the point of forgetting your Savior. Despite my bad behavior, I remembered my Savior and He delivered me once again. I found refuge at my stepmother's house, and once again, God protected me, even when I wasn't thinking about protecting myself.

Once you have accepted Jesus as your savior, you are forever apart of His royal family. I speak from first-hand knowledge when I say that God will protect you and provide refuge for you. Trust in the Lord and He will guide you through the toughest of times.

CHAPTER 5

The Bus Stops Here

A s a senior in high school, I found myself in a difficult situation. Although I had security living with Neicy, I was determined to provide for my family on my own, and this led me to resort to dishonest means in order to secure an apartment at Alexander Court, a low-income housing complex. I used Liquid Paper to change the date on my birth certificate so that I could apply for an apartment, despite being underage.

As I struggled to make ends meet, I also applied for welfare and food stamps. However, the process was humiliating and invasive, and I quickly changed my mind about accepting the assistance. Instead, I aggressively sought employment and was eventually hired as a part-time cashier at a Winn-Dixie in Toulminville. Despite the long and difficult commute using three buses, I was determined to make a better life for my son and refused to ask for help from my family or my mother. My pride and desire to prove myself led me to make poor choices and compromise my integrity, but I was convinced that it was worth it for the sake of my son and my future.

As I moved into my new apartment, I was faced with the daunting task of securing all of the necessary utilities. Despite my best efforts, I found myself unable to pay the deposit for the gas service. I was determined to handle this on my own, believing that I didn't need anyone's help. My son and I managed to get by without it, as the fall months were still mild and we didn't yet need the use of a heater. However, my baby required hot water for his bottles, and we both needed hot water for baths. I quickly realized that life often presents lemons, and I had to learn to make the best lemonade from it.

I decided to purchase a hot plate from a local pawn shop, which I used for cooking, warming my son's bottles, taking baths and for house cleaning. I was able to keep this a secret, with the hope that I would eventually be able to sell enough food stamps to eventually get the gas turned on before the winter months arrived. I also hoped to buy small decorative items to make our little apartment feel like a home.

In November, while waiting for the bus after work, a small white car pulled up and the driver, a familiar face who was one of my customers, asked if I needed a ride. As it was cold outside and it was no longer daylight savings time, riding a bus in the dark was not appealing to me. I gladly accepted the offer. His name was Butchy, and he gave me rides every day after that. He even gave me the money to finally get my gas turned on. I thought it was a nice gesture, but I didn't realize at the time that it was just the beginning of a long and difficult excursion.

I had recently started a new job at Popeye's chicken, and I had been fired from my previous job at Winn-Dixie for turning a blind eye while Butchy and his friends walked through my line without paying for cases of beer. Butchy and I were now living together, with him acting as a babysitter for my son, Jarred, on many occasions. He would pick me up from work every night and take me home. But that all changed on a cold night in December, when Butchy failed to show up to pick me up from work. The security guard was kind enough to give me a ride to pick up my baby, and then to take me home.

Pulling up to my apartment, nestled in the left corner of the street and surrounded by a towering oak tree, where neighborhood men often congregated to drink and sell drugs, I noticed Butchy's car parked outside. My back door was wide open, the blinds were all drawn up, and every light in the 1200-square-foot apartment was on. I had no idea what was going on.

Feeling uneasy, I explained my concerns to the security guard who had given me a ride home. He reassured me that he would accompany me and not to be afraid, as he had his pistol holstered to his side. As we entered the apartment through the back door, the first thing that hit me was the pungent smell of crack cocaine. Beer cans, crushed and punctured, were strewn across the kitchen countertops, table, and living room.

The security guard looked around and said, "Who lives here with you?" I replied, "Just my boyfriend, my baby, and me." He then said, "Well, someone in here is smoking crack." Right at that moment, Butchy appeared, sweating, with wide red eyes and dilated pupils, through the back door, like he had just run a marathon. He asked in a panicked tone, "What are you doing home and who is this?" referring to the security guard. I explained that the guard had given me a ride home after his failure to show up.

Butchy hesitated to answer my questions and the security guard began to leave, but not before giving me a reassuring glance that he would wait outside for a few minutes to make sure everything was okay. As I closed the blinds in my apartment and confronted Butchy about the crack cocaine accusations, I began to piece together other recent occurrences - the bulk packages of meat that went missing from the freezer, the time my wallet disappeared, and the cash and food stamps that went missing from my purse. Could it all be a result of Butchy's addiction?

I made my way to the back bedroom to close those blinds and retrieve a metal pipe that I had stashed away for protection from the neighborhood. As Butchy's voice rose and he moved closer to me, his posture and body language indicated that this would not be just another argument. Holding the pipe in my hand, I fought back as he pushed and hit me, ultimately losing the pipe to him. He then hit me with a hard blow, which landed me in my bed, alert and conscious but unable to move. I was powerless to stop him as he licked my neck, forced his tongue into my mouth and fondled my breasts. He handled me like a rag doll, taking my body and treating it like trash, all while my baby slept in his car seat in the living room.

The next morning, Butchy had left overnight, leaving my house open and unsecured. I'm not sure if my baby had even cried throughout the night, but I was awakened by my neighbor Angela, who came over to check on me. Apparently, the neighbors had heard the brawl but didn't call the police as it was a type of community where people didn't interfere or involve the police. "Tonya, who can I call," asked Angela. I could have called my stepmother and she would have been there but I wanted the love of my mother. I wanted her to nurse me back to good health. I didn't want to be just her patient; I wanted to be her daughter. I needed my mother to hold me like her baby once again. I longed for her to tell me she loved me and that I was not a failure and everything would be alright because she was there.

After my mother arrived and assessed the situation, she decided it was best for me to go to the hospital. She took me to the hospital where she was employed, and I was evaluated in the emergency room. Despite my eyes being closed, my ears were working perfectly fine. Behind the curtains, I could hear my mother telling the attendants what had happened to me. I couldn't help but feel embarrassed, especially since we had to go to the hospital where she worked. To make matters worse, I even heard her tell them to test me for drugs. I couldn't believe it, and if I hadn't been pretending to be asleep when the results came back negative, I would have jumped up and exclaimed, "Jokes on you, I don't do drugs!"

I spent the next seven days living with my mother. It was the longest seven days of my life; I heard enough "I told you so's" to last me a lifetime. I couldn't take it anymore, so on the eighth day, I returned to my apartment. Two grown women can't live together in the same house, especially when one of them has tasted freedom on the outside. When I got back to my apartment, it was a mess. The Rent-A-Center television and surround sound stereo entertainment system had been stolen from the wall. It was in my name, so I was responsible for it. I abandoned my house for a week and returned to find myself arrested for theft of property in the third degree.

Although I had not taken the property, my association with Butchy had led to my arrest. I won't mention his addiction to crack cocaine or the disgust of the rape because rape and molestation had followed me all of my life thus far, but I will reiterate that at nineteen years old, I was arrested and behind bars for a crime I did not commit. It was a blessing that in court, because I had no criminal record, the judge charged me as a youthful offender, closing all of my files publicly. However, because of my association with Butchy and my poor decision making, I was one step away from being a felon with a criminal record.

In the book of Acts, chapter 16, Paul and Silas were on their way to pray when they encountered a girl who made her living from fortune telling. She began to follow them, mocking them by saying, "These men have come to show you the way of salvation, they are servants of the Most-High God." The girl persisted in this behavior for many days, causing Paul to become annoyed with her teasing antics. Eventually, he cast the spirit of fortune telling out of her.

Upon realizing they could no longer profit from her; the girl's owners went to the magistrates to complain about Paul and Silas. This, coupled with complaints from the people of the city, led to Paul and Silas being beaten and arrested.

It is important to note that their arrest was not solely based on the casting out of the spirit from the girl, but also due to their association with Jesus Christ. Standing boldly for their beliefs ultimately led to their punishment. But, as they proclaimed the word of the Lord and praised His goodness, they were outnumbered. When one begins to praise the Lord, demons tremble in fear. In this sense, the demon inside the girl's owners was determined to destroy Paul and Silas, even if that meant lying and falsely accusing them.

Like Paul and Silas, standing for what we believe in can lead to persecution. In my own life, I was beaten by my abuser, Butchy, so badly that the hospital took pictures of my disfigured face and chipped tooth. The demon inside of him desired to take me out. But, as I learned, being chosen by God means that there is an appointed time with death and a purpose to accomplish. Even when death stares us directly in the face, we won't die because our expiration date has yet to come.

We must learn to be bold and stand against our enemies, even if it means standing alone. Some of our friends may have faced the same challenges we have faced and are no longer with us, but we are still standing. God has called us for a purpose, and we must trust in that purpose, even if it means standing alone.

In the book of II Kings, we see the story of Eleazar, a warrior chosen by David to fight against the Philistines. Despite the fact that his fellow warriors on both sides of him had abandoned the fight, Eleazar stood his ground and continued to attack the enemy. The Bible tells us in Corinthians that "God's strength is made perfect in our weakness," and in this moment, as Eleazar grew weary and his hand became frozen to his sword, the Lord was there to help him defeat the enemy and bring about a great victory.

Just like Eleazar, many of us can relate to standing alone in the face of a difficult battle. Whether it's a business venture gone awry, a failed partnership, or the struggles of single parenthood, it can feel like we're fighting alone. But just as God's strength was made perfect in Eleazar's weakness, it is in our own weaknesses that we can find the strength to continue on.

In a moment of transparency, I too have struggled with never finishing anything I've started. There were times while writing this book that I wanted to give up, that distractions slowed my progress, and that other things seemed more appealing than sitting at my desk to write. But the Holy Spirit reminded me that this battle was one of life or death, that this book would change lives, break generational curses, and that my purpose was to see it through to the end.

Just like Eleazar, we too have a job to do and a purpose to fulfill. We must not quit in the middle of the battle. I encourage you to keep your hand frozen to your sword, to stay committed to the fight, and to trust that God's strength is made perfect in your weakness.

CHAPTER 6

Keep your Foot on the Gas

Two years have passed and I am now a single mother, expecting my daughter Jazmine. I am currently living with my safe haven, Neicy, who has been there for me since the beginning. I am also working as a cook and cashier at Church's Chicken on Broad Street. Despite the long hours and the physical demands of the job, I loved every aspect of it. I took great pride in serving my customers and I had a close-knit team. It was at this job that I discovered my love for serving others.

You may be wondering how I can be satisfied with a job that pays only minimum wage and barely enough to take care of my needs. But God had great plans for me and this humble beginning was just the start.

Latonya M. Whitehead

It was at Church's Chicken that I met Big Al. He was known for his flashy appearance and his older model Honda Accord with custom rims and loud beats blasting from the trunk. His flashy exterior caught my attention, but it was his status that really caught my interest. We had a few dates, but soon it was just meetings of intimacy after work. But, as soon as my baby bump began to show, Big Al disappeared.

Just as I was about to lose hope, I met Aaron. He offered me a ride to work and soon became my daily transportation. He was kind, sweet and generous, but also easily manipulated. I took advantage of his feelings for me and used him to get what I wanted. I am ashamed of my actions towards him because he was one of the good guys, but I knew deep down that his disconnection with me was approaching as my due date was getting closer.

It was November 27, 1992, and I was scheduled to work a nine to four shift at Church's. However, by noon, I began to feel labor pains. My manager, James, insisted I leave work early, despite my reluctance as I needed every dollar of my $3.85 an hour minimum wage. I tried to reach my friend, Aaron, but was unable to, so I left work and caught the city bus. My aunt that lived in St. Stephens Woods apartments was babysitting my son and I had to ride three buses to get there. The contractions were so severe that I could barely walk. Once I arrived, I asked my aunt if I could spend the night there. She agreed, but the contractions continued throughout the night. My aunt was worried and suggested calling my mother, which we did. We both knew that the baby's time in my belly had expired and she was due at any moment.

While taking a bath, I asked my cousin, Chrissy, to call Big Al, the father of my baby. When she called him, his mother stated that he wasn't there, so I instructed her to say, "Tonya is on the way to the hospital!" His mother asked no questions, she just said, "I sure will let Big Al know," and ended the call.

My mother arrived to escort me to the hospital to deliver my first baby girl. However, because I had not dilated enough, we were playing the waiting game. With around the clock nursing support, my family came in and out of the room, two at a time, one on each side of my bed. My Granny and Papa came first, with tears in their eyes as they began to touch and pray with me. I didn't understand why I was getting so much attention; this didn't happen when I had my first baby. Soon after, my other aunts and uncles came in two at a time, telling me how much they loved me and that everything would be alright. Finally, the last two to enter my bedside were Aaron and Big Al. Aaron, holding my hand with tears falling from his eyes, down his cheek to the sheet on the hospital bed. Aaron began tell me he loved me; while Big Al, stood to the left of me with no words at all, just looking at the fool of a man crying over his baby's mother.

Suddenly, the loud sounds of beeping machinery began to ignite the room from every direction! The nurse began to call for help as she insisted Aaron and Big Al leave the room immediately! In ran a few more nurses! Flipping me over to my hands and knees just like the emergency room movies except, I didn't hear anyone yell, "STAT!" They were prying and pushing in my stomach and all of my private parts! I began to cry! Everything was happening so fast! They were pushing and pulling and all I could do in tears was ask, "what is going on?" Finally, the nurse explains, "I was losing my baby." My sweet little princess had little heart beat due to the umbilical cord being wrapped around her neck choking her lifeless. My baby was dying! In minutes they prepped me for an emergency C-section.

While rolling me down the hall on the hospital bed, the nurse said, "LaTonya the baby's grandmother will be in the operating room with you." I heard what she said but I assumed she was talking about my mother; besides, prior to this day, I had never met or spoken to anyone in Big Al's family.

As I lay on the operating table, preparing for the arrival of my baby girl, I was surprised to see that my mother was not present in the operating room. Instead, I saw a woman dressed in a yellow hospital gown, wearing gloves, a mask, and a cap, with glasses perched on her nose. It was only when she began to rub my hand and assure me that everything would be fine that I realized it was Big Al's mother. As I looked at her, I could see a resemblance to her and Big Al.

As the doctors worked to bring my baby into the world, I watched through the mirror above the doctor's head as Jazmine was pulled from my stomach. In a moment of pure relief, I heard her cries and knew that she was perfect. She weighed over eight pounds and had beautiful, curly hair. She was the first grandbaby girl on both sides of her family, just like me.

After having the C-section, my hospital stay was longer than expected due to daily fevers. Aaron, my friend was a constant presence, visiting me every day; However, one day, Big Al came to the hospital unannounced and, upon seeing Aaron holding and rocking Jazmine, he politely took her out of his hands. This was a very awkward moment, as I was forced to sit with both Jazmine's father and the man who desired to be her father. To make matters worse, my mother arrived and told me to "send Aaron home, he does not belong here." My mother was not aware of the extent of Aaron's and my relationship. She didn't understand all the times Aaron aided me with meals throughout my pregnancy. She had no idea about the doctor appointments he transported me to when I had no ride, but I was easily persuaded when she explained that Big Al was trying to bond with his daughter and pursue a lost relationship with me. I asked Aaron to leave, breaking his heart and causing him great pain.

Two days later, my doctor declared that I could go home, as long as my baby had a car seat and I had no fever over the next twenty-four hours. I was thrilled to be leaving the hospital after a week-long stay. Still without a stable home, I made plans to return to Neicy's after I had already been jumping from house to house, staying with anybody but just long enough to not wear away my welcome. In the days leading up to my discharge, Aaron had been calling me at the hospital, and I had been talking to him occasionally. However, when Big Al was present, I ignored his calls.

As I prepared to leave the hospital, I received a delivery of beautiful red roses. The roses were in a tall, crystal vase with a white bow, but there was no card attached. I had no idea who had sent them. My daughter's aunt, Christine, arrived to shower Jazmine with pretty pink and yellow outfits, matching bows, and shoes.

As Christine prepared to leave, I suddenly began to cough uncontrollably. The strong smell of fumes in the air made me feel nauseous, dizzy, and weak. It became clear that the source of the smell was the arrangement of roses in my hospital room. Christine quickly called her mother, my mother, and her brother, Big Al to alert them of the situation. To everyone's surprise, the fumes were only affecting me.

The hospital staff was alerted and after taking my temperature, it was determined that I had another fever and my blood pressure was rising. This setback would delay my discharge from the hospital. After much speculation, it was concluded that the bouquet had been sent by Aaron with the intent of harming me and my baby. Despite my initial doubts, I went along with this being the family's assumption.

As a result, my mother forbade me from speaking to Aaron and instructed me to tell him to never call me again or face harassment charges. I obediently followed her instructions and hung up on him every time he called the hospital.

54

On my last night in the hospital, Aaron suddenly appeared, panting and out of breath, claiming that he had run past security to see me and declare his love for me and his desire to be Jazmine's father. I attempted to explain that Jazmine already had a father, but before I could finish, security knocked on my door. To protect Aaron from getting into trouble, he hid in the closet and I lied and told them he had just left.

After security left, I insisted that Aaron leave and never return. I did not want him to get into any more trouble. Despite his pleas of love, he eventually left my room. I was now under around-the-clock security surveillance, feeling like a celebrity, but with no one able to visit me. I was unsure of who had arranged for the added security, but I was left to spend my final hours at the University of South Alabama Hospital with the security but without the luxury of television service since they charged $3 a day for it; I could not afford to pay for it.

After all that had happened, you might be wondering how Big Al and I managed to become a couple and eventually get married. Unfortunately, the reality was not as glamorous as you might have imagined. Following my hospital release, Big Al and I saw each other very infrequently. He failed to deliver on promises of diapers, formula, and even visitation. Like many other single mothers, I faced numerous struggles, such as when the W.I.C. program didn't provide enough milk for my big, healthy baby. To make matters worse, Jazmine couldn't drink regular Similac or Enfamil; she had to have a special type of goat milk that was hard to find and very expensive. But, as the saying goes, "God always makes a way."

This reminds me of the story of the Shunammite woman in I Kings chapter 17. She was a widow with one child, and the Spirit of the Lord told Elijah to go to her house because she was going to feed him. When Elijah arrived, he asked her for a drink of water and some bread. The woman replied that she only had a handful of flour and a little olive oil in a jar, and that she was going to make a meal for herself and her son to eat before they died of starvation. Elijah then instructed her to make a loaf of bread for him first, and promised that from that day forward she would never run out of flour or oil again. Through her obedience and faith, God provided for her and her son.

Similarly, throughout my struggles as a single mother, God was always there to guide and provide for me, even if I couldn't see it at the time. There were moments when I didn't understand why things were happening the way they were, and I made poor decisions as a result. But, looking back, I realize that God was trying to teach me maturity and faith. It's true that, if I had known then what I know now, things might have been different, but, ultimately, I credit everything to God's purpose.

God wants to be our spiritual guide, leading us through the unknown path of life and protecting us from unseen dangers. However, there are times when we tend to put on spiritual blindfolds and attempt to do things our own way without consulting the Father for instructions or guidance.

Imagine you are traveling through an unfamiliar area using a GPS. You may miss a turn or make a wrong one, but the GPS will recalculate your directions and give you an alternate route. Similarly, in life, it is fine to make a mistake or miss an exit. What is not okay is turning off the engine in the middle of the street and giving up. This is the time to adjust your course and press on.

For single parents, divorcees, and entrepreneurs, now is not the time to give up. Keep moving forward, even when things seem hopeless. The Shunammite woman was preparing to die before the man of God appeared. She had lost all hope, but she was blessed for being disciplined and obedient enough to honor what God had said.

If you feel called to a specific assignment but are hesitant to move forward, remember that your purpose cannot be fulfilled until God's will becomes a priority. To understand your purpose, you must first learn to pray and ask God for it. Then, you must listen in obedience to his instructions and be disciplined enough to follow through. Keep your foot on the gas and trust that God will guide you to your destination.

CHAPTER 7

Don't Lose Your Strength

As I reach my twenty-third birthday, I can't help but reflect on the path that has led me to where I am today - a mother of two. It's hard to believe how quickly time has passed and how drastically my life has changed.

Two years ago, I became involved with Scott. We shared a home, made plans for marriage and starting a family together. But as the saying goes, "if you want to make God laugh, tell him your plans." Our relationship, which once seemed unbreakable, was shattered by Scott's infidelity.

The first time it happened, I forgave him, convinced that it was a one-time mistake. But the betrayal continued, each time more painful than the last. The final straw came when I returned home unexpectedly and found Scott in bed with another woman - someone I knew from my job at Church's

Chicken. I was four months pregnant with my youngest child, J'Kala.

Enraged, heartbroken, and keyless, I attempted to break down the door to my own home. As I held a crowbar in a baseball swing position, when the door suddenly swung open. Scott stood there, shirtless and in his underwear, looking like a deer caught in headlights. He had the audacity to ask me what I was doing home?

I pushed past him to find the woman's purse sitting on my coffee table. As I made my way through the living room, I could smell her perfume and see the evidence of her presence in my bedroom. The bathroom door was closed and locked, but with one powerful kick, I broke it down to find the woman half-dressed and claiming ignorance of me and Scott's relationship.

How could she not know? Our family portraits were displayed prominently throughout the house. What lies had Scott told her to convince her to stay, undress, and lie in my bed? How could he do this to me, especially when I was pregnant with his child? I trusted him and he had made so many promises of marriage and a better life together. But those promises meant nothing in the face of his infidelity.

Despite the pain and betrayal, I stayed with Scott. I couldn't bear the thought of having another child without their father being present, especially since I already had two children without their dads. After J'Kala was born, it was challenging and embarrassing to have to explain to people that they all had different fathers. I felt ashamed and feared judgment, so I began to tell little white lies, saying that my oldest two children had the same father.

Scott and I struggled emotionally and financially. He had three children from previous relationships and child support was taking a significant portion of his paychecks. In retrospect, I regret not having my best interests at heart and staying with a man who pretended to love me while loving other women behind my back. The signs were there all along, but I made excuses for him and even laughed it off when I saw him staring at other women in my presence. Life is a constant lesson, and sometimes we have to fail miserably and repeat the same mistakes before we finally reach our breaking point.

In the Book of Judges, chapter 16, we read the story of Samson and his ill-fated love for Delilah. Samson was a man of great strength, gifted by God, and had defeated many of his enemies on his own. However, the Philistines, his mortal foes, sought to eliminate him and thus, they enlisted Delilah's help in discovering the source of his strength so they could render him powerless and kill him. Delilah was promised a large sum of money in return for her assistance.

Delilah began her scheme by simply asking Samson, "How can you be tied up and subdued?" Samson, however, lied to her on three different occasions, which led Delilah to feel foolish and her attempts to capture him failed. Each time she asked, "What would make you weak?" Delilah had help from the Philistines to plan his downfall by capturing him once his strength was gone.

Despite their failed attempts, Delilah continued to manipulate and charm Samson with her words, saying "If you loved me, you would tell me where your strength lies." Eventually, Samson, unable to resist Delilah's spell, revealed to her, "My strength lies within my hair, if cut, I will be as weak as any other man." Once Delilah realized that Samson had honestly shared his secret, she called for the Philistines. While Samson slept on her lap, Delilah cut his hair and the Philistines were able to subdue him, binding him with shackles, gouging out his eyes, and making him their captive.

Samson, like the protagonist in the story, failed to recognize Delilah's true character and intentions even after she had deceived him three times. He was so enamored with her that he failed to see her true identity. Similarly, in my own life, my partner Scott had shown me his true character each time he was unfaithful. Like Samson, I constantly believed I could trust him, even when I was deceived. Each time I opened my heart to him, he betrayed me, ultimately cheating one final time.

In the Book of Romans, chapter 12:2, the Word of God speaks about the importance of not conforming to the ways of the world, but instead being transformed by the renewing of one's mind. This message resonated with me deeply as I struggled with feelings of loneliness, fear, and embarrassment as a single parent of three children with three different fathers. I

Latonya M. Whitehead

knew that in order to move forward and create a better future for my children and myself, my mind and soul needed to be healed and transformed.

I began to seek out God's plan for my life, and I found myself working harder than ever before. I transferred from working at Church's Chicken on Broad to becoming an assistant at the St. Stephen Road location. It was there that I began to build my confidence and character, and I enjoyed the opportunity to train, develop, and lead others. My hard work paid off when the Manager from the adjacent Kentucky Fried Chicken asked me to leave Church's to work as an assistant for her. Despite feeling a sense of betrayal, I accepted the job and remained a part-time team member at Church's.

As I continued to work hard, I enrolled in classes to become a Certified Nursing Assistant. After completing my courses, I was hired at Fairhope Nursing Home as a C.N.A. I was determined to provide the best for my children, so I decided to enroll in nursing school full-time. However, my newfound drive and determination were met with challenges as I struggled to balance full-time school with working the third shift as a C.N.A. at Cogburn Nursing Home. Despite my best efforts, I found myself failing Anatomy twice and being placed on academic probation. Faced with these obstacles, I gave up and quit.

Looking back, I realize that I stopped in the middle of God's positioning for my purpose. I was too afraid to face failure and too apprehensive to stare down obstacles, but I also know that

God's plan for me is not over and that He will continue to lead me towards my purpose.

Listen, achieving one's purpose in life is not an easy task. It requires a great deal of commitment and discipline. But there will be times when the road ahead seems difficult and uncertain. What do you do in those moments? Let me tell you the story of Zacchaeus and what he did.

Zacchaeus was a wealthy tax collector, but in the eyes of many, he was also a sinner. He wanted to see Jesus, but because of his short stature and the large crowd, he couldn't see him. So, Zacchaeus got creative and climbed a sycamore fig tree to catch a glimpse of Jesus as he passed. And when Jesus reached the spot where Zacchaeus was, he looked up and called him down from the tree, inviting himself to stay at Zacchaeus' house. The crowd murmured and criticized Jesus for going to the house of a sinner, but Zacchaeus stood tall and committed to giving half of his possessions to the poor and making restitution for any wrongs he had committed. And Jesus declared that salvation had come to Zacchaeus' house that day.

This story teaches us that when we encounter Jesus, our lives can change in an instant. Just like Zacchaeus, we all have the ability to finish what we started, even when things get hard. We must remember our dreams, our goals, and the person that God created us to be. And when our vision becomes clouded, we must look higher, further, and even climb a sycamore tree if necessary. Remember, just one visit with

Latonya M. Whitehead

Jesus can bring deliverance, peace, hope, and freedom. Today is the day of salvation, and it's not too late for you to achieve your purpose and experience the same change that Zacchaeus did. Don't give up, look for your sycamore tree, and let Jesus stay in your house today.

CHAPTER 8

The Stranger in My House

After seven long years of being on a waiting list, I was finally approved for Section 8, a government-funded housing assistance program. With this program, I was able to secure a two-bedroom house or apartment based on my income. Despite having a decent job, I still struggled financially. However, things were starting to look up.

The timing couldn't have been more perfect, as I had recently received my income tax check and was able to purchase new furnishings for my new two-bedroom townhouse on Navco Road. I was also able to buy my first car from a "buy here, pay here" lot. My finances, focus and singleness were beginning to align, as I worked hard and focused on being an awesome parent.

Life was finally starting to feel balanced. I wasn't dating anyone, my children were involved in little league sports, and

I no longer had to rely on others for rides to work or the grocery store. I was even able to afford to visit the hair salon a few times a month. Every Friday, after clocking out from work at two, I would take the drive from Eastern Shore Nursing Home to Toulminville, where my God-sister, Monica, would make me feel gorgeous by styling my hair to perfection.

But it wouldn't be long before I found myself back in the familiar rut of struggling to pay my bills, having financial hardships, and entangled in a relationship with a man. One day, while in the salon, a man entered and began talking to the owner, charming the rest of us with his jokes, northern accent, and cute dimpled face. Little did I know that his presence in the salon would lead to an embroiled relationship full of downfalls, lies, cheating, and scandalous behavior.

The next Friday, while in the salon, my stylist told me that the gentleman from the previous week had an interest in meeting me and suggested I call him. Without hesitation, I called and we arranged to meet in person at the salon. As we all chatted, my stylist realized she needed a few items to complete my hair do and Terry, the charming man from Detroit, accompanied me to the beauty supply store. As we drove down the busy Airport Boulevard, I learned that he was new to the area, living with his father, and looking for change and a way to stay out of trouble. I was intrigued and eager to learn more about him, which led to our next date.

One week later, Terry and I found ourselves at a local club downtown. It was only my second time ever being in a night club, and I couldn't help but feel out of place. I hadn't dressed as revealing as the other women there because I didn't have any club clothes, and I didn't feel like I belonged. Despite my discomfort, Terry's stares into my eyes, made me feel like I was the only woman in the room. I found that even though I felt awkward, I enjoyed dancing and music.

After a few drinks, Terry and I headed back to my place. I wanted to show him my new, unfurnished townhouse, with the hope that it would pique his interest. I also convinced him to help me put up the mini blinds, which I didn't have yet. That night, as we looked at my new place, we ended up in the upstairs bedroom, where we passionately kissed and made love on the floor of that empty, cold apartment.

The next morning, as the bright sunshine streamed into our faces, I wondered would this be a one-night stand. Despite any clarity, I drove Terry home. During the drive, he revealed that he would be leaving for a new job for a few weeks, and we would resume our time together upon his return. While he was away, I had the opportunity to get my place together. Once my new furniture arrived, I had everything I needed for our new place, except a television. It was fine though, because once the kids got in from school, football and cheerleading practice, it was homework, baths and bedtime, so they really didn't miss what they didn't have.

A few weeks later, Terry was back, and I couldn't wait for him to see the fully furnished facelift of the place. And the next day, he surprised me by buying us a television. I suspect he loved my cooking and home décor so much, that he never left. I had moved this man into my house, without truly knowing who he really was. I was so desperate for a relationship that I allowed a stranger into my house. This stranger would ultimately become my husband, but looking back, I see the risk associated with my compromise. I realize now that my poor decision-making could have been detrimental. This misjudgment could have landed me back in familiar territory of low self-esteem and feeling not good enough. At twenty-six, I couldn't recognize this as my pattern.

It was a typical Saturday evening and I was working my second job at the local video store, determined to never return to my former life of struggle. I had been fortunate enough to secure a second job as a customer service representative to supplement my income. My boyfriend, Terry, was employed by the labor union and made great money when he worked, but his assignments were often short-lived, lasting a few weeks to a couple of months. This meant that he would be drawing unemployment until his name resurfaced at the top of the working list again.

As I was stocking the shelves at the video store, a police officer walked into the store and approached me. "Are you LaTonya?" he asked. "Do you have children that live at 805 Navco Road?" My heart sank as I nodded yes, afraid of what he was going to say next. The officer told me that he had received calls stating that my children were left home unattended and that drugs were present in the house. I protested, insisting that my boyfriend, Terry, was home watching my kids and that there were no drugs present in the house.

The officer then spoke into his handheld radio, updating dispatch on the situation. He turned back to me and said, "I was not supposed to come here, but when your son opened the door, he was very mannered and polite. Your house was clean and there were no signs of drug activity. I knew then that someone was just trying to cause you problems by calling us to take your kids."

Feeling relieved but still shaken, I quickly turned off the lights, locked up the video store and called my boss to explain the unfortunate situation and my immediate departure. I didn't have my car, so I had to ride in the back of the police car, feeling like I had been placed under arrest. The officer became my chauffeur, driving me back to my house. As we drove, I couldn't help but think about how close I had come to losing my children and how desperate my situation had become. I knew that I needed to make some changes in my life to ensure the safety and well-being of my family, but I didn't know how. Terry had become my only source.

As I opened the door to my house, I was met with a heart-wrenching sight. My children were huddled on the living room floor, crying desperately for their mother. Jarred, my eldest, explained to me that their grandmother had just left and had threatened to have them taken away. I couldn't believe that my own mother could be so cruel. What could have possibly motivated her to do this to me and my children? To make matters worse, she had to pass by my job, located at the corner of Navco and Pleasant Valley, on her way to her house. It was clear to me that my mother was completely unconcerned for the well-being of my children that day. I couldn't help but feel that the enemy was using her in an attempt to destroy me.

I was livid, and since I didn't have a cell phone at the time, I marched, like Sophia did in the Color Purple, when asking Mister, "You told Harpo to beat Me?" The march was to the corner gas station to call my mother. I asked her, "How could you do this? How could you try to take my children away from me, especially after what you went through with my stepfather in the custody battle over my little brother? You should know how this feel!" My mother had no response, and I ended the call with, "I will never speak to you again."

In hindsight, I realize that my mother's actions were not justified, and neither was my outburst. The word of God in Ephesians 6:1-3 tells us that as children, we should obey our parents and honor them in order for our days to be long. At the time, my relationship with my mother was characterized by my rebellion, disagreements, and disrespect. Dishonoring her did not elevate me in any way; it only revealed my lack of character. We must understand that dishonoring someone, especially our parents, will only create a larger gap and will not change the other person.

Ephesians 6 gives us a two-step process for a longer life: obedience as the foundation and honor as the key to the reward. It was painful for me to go months without speaking to my mother. I needed her, in so many ways but my pride kept me from saying "I'm sorry." My selfishness caused me to not speak to my mother for almost two years. I can only imagine the regret I would have felt if the Lord had called her home during that time. This is a story that I may explore in another book.

Engaged to Terry, my now husband, we had recently moved into a beautiful brick home at 270 Magnolia Drive in Toulminville. The house was perfect for our growing family, with huge front and back yards, an outside brick fire pit with a covered patio, a built-in fireplace, four bedrooms, den, dining, living, and family rooms. It was everything we had imagined, except for one thing: we were renting it through section 8 and, because of the size and beauty of this house, we didn't realize we were living in the ghetto, a less-than-desirable neighborhood.

You see, Terry and I had a problem. We were "ghetto-fabulous", and we loved to entertain. We would have parties, couples game nights, pay-per-view fights and wrestling matches, while inviting friends and family. To make matters worse, Terry was a habitual club-goer. His club schedule consisted of Blue Monday, Two-Dollar Tuesday, Wicked

Wednesday's, and Ladies Night Thursday. Fridays were designated as date night for me, which usually ended up being dinner with the kids at Quincy's on Moffat Road, filling up on the buttery yeast rolls.

Don't get me wrong, there is nothing wrong with entertaining and breaking bread with friends and family, but the problem arose when the two of us didn't have two quarters to rub together to make fifty cents afterwards. No one knew that our lights were being turned off after all the parties and pay-per-view events of The Roc and Stone Cold. We couldn't tell them that after we pay-per-viewed Mike Tyson and Larry Holmes, the next day we had no water. We were pretending to be something we were not. We were imitations of Jay-Z and Beyoncé, just call us Jay-T and Teyoncé. We both had been fooled and tricked by the facade of the big house we were renting. We were tricked by the fame of looking like big shots, we were even misled by thinking we were more than our friends. If only they knew the real struggle.

Terry and I were married on March 4, 2000. I was the happiest woman in the world. Who would have thought that a man without children would want to marry me, a woman with three kids? We lived in a big house; Terry was driving an old nineteen sixty-six Pontiac Tempest, (courtesy of my nineteen ninety-nine tax return), we had Debo, the rottweiler that guarded the yard, and I finally had a male figure in the home for my kids. However, one of the biggest misconceptions that many women have learned was taken from a song entitled, "No Pain, No Gain." In this song, Miss Betty says, "having a piece of man is better than having no man at all." This concept leads me to believe that regardless of the man's behavior, intent, integrity, how bad he is for you, or how bad he makes you feel as a woman; it is acceptable to keep him; for it is better to have him than no man at all! Sisters, wake up! I endured cheating from this man, I subjected myself to a continuation of lies, deceit, and heartbreak. The similar cycle from past relationships continued to gravitate to me. I thought I could do no better because I only had a high school education, a single mother with three children, all with different fathers, I was skinny, with no rear end, a flat chest, and I was ugly. Who else would want me? I thought this man was my only hope at marriage, love and happiness.

It was around the summer of 2006 when I decided to get my hair braided with weave. One weekend night, my husband Terry was out clubbing as usual. Being my first-time getting braids, I didn't anticipate the process taking as long as it did. I called home repeatedly, asking my son, Jarred, if Terry had been looking for me. Eventually, I returned home five hours later with long braids cascading down my back.

It was 4 a.m. when Terry finally came home. He regaled me with a graphic account of the night's events at Club Brandi's. He claimed that our neighbors had gotten into a fight and that he had had to step in to stop it, protecting three women in the process. He said he was going back to check on them. I insisted on accompanying him to check on the women, but Terry was not happy about it.

Latonya M. Whitehead

When I arrived at Stephanie's house, her friend showed me to the kitchen where Stephanie was cooking breakfast. She ignored me as though I were invisible, which took me by surprise since I had never been in her house before. When I asked her about the fight and if everyone was okay, she looked confused and denied any knowledge of a fight. Her version of events was vastly different from Terry's account. She said he had been buying drinks for them all evening and seemed to have had expectations of a good time with one or all of them by the end of the night.

Feeling disappointed and betrayed, I thanked Stephanie for her honesty and headed back home to confront Terry. I asked him why he lied and what his intentions were? Was it the alcohol that Jamie Foxx sings about that made him act this way? Whatever the reason, his actions led to a physical altercation between us and my newly installed braids were pulled and used like a lasso as a means of control.

As the sun began to rise behind the trees, the sounds of yelling, screaming, and cursing filled the air. The kids were awakened by the ruckus as my husband and I fought fiercely outside on the porch and in the yard. The fighting became so intense that I heard the sirens of the approaching police cars. My husband, Terry, was sitting in his car trying to escape, but I barricaded him from leaving. I knew he needed to be held accountable for his actions, for hitting and hurting me. I wouldn't let him hit and run.

When the police arrived, I stepped aside and away from Terry. Like a scene from a TV show, they proceeded to tell him to step out of the car with his hands up. But to our shock, Terry stepped out with a gun! The police, neighboring bystanders, and I all yelled for him to put the gun down, but he looked as though he was possessed. He was in such a rage and ready to meet his maker that day. The police all had weapons drawn and he was surrounded. Thank God this was then and not today.

After many yells and pleas, he finally threw the gun down and began to demand the police to "fight him like a man!" As the four officers attempted to subdue Terry, he fought them like a madman out of control. I didn't know what had gotten into my husband. He had never acted so out of control and enraged. Finally, the police were able to place him on the ground, put him in handcuffs, and read him his Miranda rights. He was released on bond the next day and back at home with me.

Let me clear up a misconception that many of us ladies may have. Having sex will not, does not, cannot, and never has healed an issue. Sex is not a solution. Anytime sex is done wrongly, it will be the problem! During a sexual act, your emotions are high and uncontrollable. You will be fooled to think that the problem is resolved, but in all actuality, the problem has just begun. Terry and I went through all of that and ended up forgetting what happened just twenty-four hours ago. We put that little incident behind us and faced even bigger incidents from it.

Latonya M. Whitehead

Terry was now being sought by the US Marshalls for being a felon in possession of a lethal weapon. That gun that night had him facing almost twenty years in federal prison. After turning himself in and going to court, he was sentenced to eighteen months in a prison in Arkansas. During this time, I knew there had to be a change. I was grown so tired of my dysfunction. I wanted to learn about God and seek the Lord for my family. My husband needed a praying wife, and my children needed a praying mother. I didn't know where to start, but the God I serve had it all lined up.

Going to see Monica at the hair salon, I remembered the owner, Melissa, always talking about the goodness of God. She was always praying, singing, and exuding a persona that was full of life. She would often plant seeds of wisdom in me, and one day, she invited me to visit her church, which I nicknamed "The Rock".

This small storefront church, located on Dr. Martin Luther King Jr. Boulevard, packed a powerful punch. From the moment I walked through the front door and was greeted by the ushers, to the flow of the service led by the choir that sounded like a record deal, and the pastor's preaching, I was hooked. His messages about Jesus Christ were filled with humor, tears, intellect, hope, and the Spirit of God. I continued to go back Sunday after Sunday, getting filled with the word of God. I wanted change and this was it.

Not having any church clothes to adjust to my new-found lifestyle, I asked my aunt, who we all call Nanny, who was also a few sizes larger than I, if I could borrow some clothes from her closet. She always wore the top brands from Belk and Dillards, so I knew I would get only the best from her. After scavenging through her closet, I found five suits that were all too big. We discussed the need to alter them before wearing them, but I couldn't wait, church was in a few days, and I desired to look sanctified and it would start this Sunday.

My plan was to wear the purple suit with the gold buttons, my nude stockings, and tiny black heels. I told myself, "No one would recognize the suit being two sizes too big because I would show up late, sit in the back, and not move a muscle until the service was over and immediately run to my car without any fellowship!" But the Holy Ghost had other plans.

As the pastor was preaching and sweating, the Spirit was in the room! Jeffery was on the piano, Quinton on the keyboard, Jason on the bass, and Shawn on the drums. When they hit that one note, fire shot through my little bones, and I could not stop running circles around the sanctuary! After about ten laps, I finally stopped, but I was jumping, screaming, speaking in tongues, all in front of the church at the pulpit! I knew where I was, but I was staggering from a Holy Ghost high. The Spirit of the Lord hit me that day, and I was unembarrassed. That was the day I joined the ministry with the too-big purple suit that everyone could now see. Not only did I join, but I began to work; singing in the choir, drama ministry, the youth department under Carol, and the women's praise dance team. I really appreciate Vanessa for being so patient with me and my two left feet, while trying to dance to Natalie Wilson's Free.

It was now almost two years later, when I was at the prison in Arkansas to receive Terry after his release. I was sure the marriage would now take a turn for the better, especially after all the letters, costly phone calls, money being added to his commissary, and me taking those long eight-hour drives to visit him. Nevertheless, our marriage was now worse than it had ever been. My husband continued to disrespect me, stay out all night, coming home just in time to change his clothes for work, and repeating the same scenario again tomorrow. Even though I was starting to be stronger in the Lord, I accepted what my husband had to give because I thought that was all I deserved. I was okay with the "piece of man" Betty spoke of. I was fine loving a man that obviously didn't love me. I stayed despite my husband, being the stranger in my house.

As the days passed, Terry and I grew increasingly distant, like oil and water unable to mix. I, feeling like Annie Mae from the movie; What Love Got to Do with It, began to be an angry black woman, mad at my husband and furious with God for allowing me to endure such pain. I had always been a good girl. I made sure Terry's house was clean, I ran his bath water, I kept his stomach full, I paid the bills, I prayed and went to church. I couldn't understand why God would allow this to happen to me. I had always been willing to help others, and now I felt like I had no husband to help me. Why didn't Terry demonstrate the love for me that God commands for all husbands in Ephesians 5:25? Why would I expect him to show me love when he had never seen or experienced it himself? He too had been a victim of abuse and manipulation by the man he called "Mister," when enticed by alcohol.

To those of you whose love language is acts of service, like mine, be cautious when entering into a relationship. Our willingness to give and take action can often blind us to the warning signs. It took me a lot of soul searching, staring in the mirror, long rides in the car, and many tears in my closet, along with God's deliverance, before I was able to face the truth. The truth was, my issues were a direct result of my actions. My selfishness and cravings had led me down this path.

But there is hope. In the book of Jeremiah, God gives a message of hope. "I knew you before I formed you in your mother's womb. Before you were born, I set you apart and appointed you as my prophet to the nations." Listen, men and women of God, you are Jeremiah! God knew you, created you with purpose, and set you apart before you were born. But we must not be ignorant to Satan's devices, which can distract us from God's will for our lives. I was in the right place at the right time, but I allowed the enemy to blindside me with things that detached me from God's purpose for my life.

God, your creator, wants you to understand why you were designed and what your purpose is in his Kingdom. If your iPhone malfunctions, you wouldn't go to Samsung for a fix, because only the creator of the iPhone (Apple) knows how it was built. Only the creator knows what is placed on the inside. The same is true for you - you were born with purpose in mind, chosen to do a specific thing so that God's Kingdom can be glorified. Despite all the trials, tribulations, heartache and heartbreak, your purpose still awaits you. Go to your creator, only he knows what he has placed inside of you.

CHAPTER 9

Life After Death

It all started with my failing marriage to Terry. As we struggled to hold our relationship together, I found solace in my work as a construction worker in Theodore. It was there that I met Steven, a fellow married man with whom I struck up an innocent friendship. We spent our breakfasts and lunches together, swapping stories of the marriages we had always dreamed of. We both longed for the kind of partner we saw in each other - he admired my strength and resilience, while I envied his devoted love and attention.

But as our friendship deepened, we began to crave more of each other's company. So, when a rainout at the construction site sent us home early one day, we seized the opportunity to take a trip to the bowling alley together. It was a weekday, so there were hardly any people around to witness our secret rendezvous. As we laughed and joked, I couldn't help but imagine what it would be like to be with a man like Steven.

Latonya M. Whitehead

As the demon whispered in my ear, reminding me of my failures and my worthlessness, I was content with the void being filled by Steven.

After our first date, Steven and I began to further our relationship by engaging in an adulterous affair, sneaking kisses whenever we could at work. Our lack of cohesion was palpable, and it led to me leaving home while my husband went out to the clubs, slipping into easy access mini- skirts or dresses as soon as he was out of the house. I never feared being caught, as I knew my husband would be out until the early hours of the morning, but Steven and I never stayed out that long. I was always home, showered, and back in bed before my husband ever noticed.

I, LaTonya, now wore the scarlet letter "A" on my shirt, having committed the ultimate sin. I had never cheated on my husband before, and at the time, I didn't feel guilty, ashamed, embarrassed, or remorseful about it. I believed my husband deserved it. These crossroads had me facing the human conflict between emotion and intellect. My intelligence knew that cheating was not the right thing to do, but my emotions of feeling loved, wanted, and needed had me entangled and going back for more.

As Steven and I spent more time together, we even allowed our children to meet and have playdates, disguising our affair as mere work friends. But our children saw through our facade, they saw the way Steven looked at me and the way I smiled back at him. However, our tangled web of lust and deceit would eventually unravel.

As I continued to go to church and learn more about God's grace and mercy, my heart began to change. Even though I had one foot in the church and the other out, almost in a backslidden state, I still stayed at the altar for prayer. After a while, I began to lose the desire to have another man do what I longed for my husband to do. In my prayers, I began to ask God to remove the things that were not like him, but ultimately, I had to make a choice by letting go of the things that did not align with His Biblical principles. If I wanted to live a saved and holy life, it would not be easy. It took days of trying to ignore Steven at work, not meeting him at his car for breakfast, and even missing him so much that I met him at lunch where we hid behind tents for a sexual quicky. I was trying my best to stop seeing him, but it was so hard. My flesh craved his touch. He was like a drug calling me back for another high. But with God's help, I was able to break free from this unhealthy relationship.

As I arrived at the construction site one morning, our foreman was conducting a safety meeting and handing out pink layoff slips. With my fingers crossed, I stood among my colleagues, all hoping that our names would not be called next. Fortunately, I was not served a pink slip but my friend, Steven received one and was sent home that day. I watched him walk slowly to his car, disappointment etched on his face, as he smiled and thanked Melvin for the opportunity.

On one hand, I was disheartened by Steven's loss of job, but on the other hand, a small part of me was relieved knowing that his absence would eventually fade from my mind. Despite this, Steven and I continued to have telephone conversations over the next few days. However, I would often excuse myself from these calls due to a lack of prepaid minutes on my cellphone. Steven would always try to convince me to stay on the line by offering to add more time, but I always declined, pretending to be a concerned friend, saying "No, you should save your money now that you're not working." Each time, Steven would agree, but also reminded me of how much he missed me and hoped for a secret car meeting. But I never agreed to these terms, as my interest in him had begun to wane. The encounters we had before were just momentary pleasure, leaving me feeling empty and unfulfilled.

I couldn't help but compare my interactions with Steven to a full course meal. Just as a full course meal, such as a T-bone steak, loaded baked potato, and salad, leaves you feeling full and nourished, my encounters with Steven only left me feeling temporarily satisfied, but ultimately unfulfilled. As Jesus says in John 6:35, "I am the bread of life. Whoever comes to me will never be hungry, and whoever believes in me shall never be thirsty." Jesus' words and actions remind us that it is not enough to simply fill our bodies with food, we must also be spiritually fed through the word of God. And so, I knew that in order to truly move on from Steven, I had to change my mind and heart. I had to include fasting in my praying and deny my fleshly desires. I had to stop watching movies and listening to love songs that reminded me of him. Only then was I able to allow the Holy Spirit to do the rest. However, my journey was not without its struggles, as Steven was not willing to give up without a fight.

As I reflect on my dining experiences, I cannot recall a single instance where I have finished a full course meal without feeling quenched. A classic example would be the dinner consisting of a T-boned steak, a loaded baked potato, and a salad. Upon completion, one may find themselves feeling full and possibly not having any room for dessert. However, if one were to replace this meal with a bowl of ice cream, although the sensation of fullness may be present, it is not accompanied by any substantial nourishment or sustenance. The ice cream, lacking in solidity and nutritional value, temporarily fills the stomach but ultimately leaves one feeling empty. This analogy can be applied to other aspects of life, as temporary pleasures may provide temporary satisfaction but ultimately leave one feeling unfulfilled.

Even though, being with Steven repleted me for a time, shortly after I was depleted once again. In the Book of John, chapter 6:35, Jesus declares, *"I am the bread of life. Whoever comes to me will never be hungry and whoever believes in me shall never be thirsty.* Jesus' words and actions remind us that it is not enough to simply fill our bodies with food, we must also be spiritually fed through the word of God. And so, I knew that in order to truly move on from Steven, I had to change my mind and heart. I had to include fasting in my praying and deny my fleshly desires. I had to stop watching movies and listening to love songs that reminded me of him. Only then was I able to allow the Holy Spirit to do the rest. However, my journey was not without its struggles, as Steven was not willing to give up without a fight.

It was a typical Friday night for me. I had just finished ironing my husband, Terry's club outfit, watching him dress, spraying on cologne and adding his wedding ring to his attire. He kissed me on the cheek and said, "I'll be back," as he locked the door behind him.

But things took a turn for the unexpected when the landline telephone rang a few minutes later. To my surprise, it was Steven, the old acquaintance who was attempting to reenter my life. He asked me, "Can you come out and play?" I replied, "No, I can't. He's home," as I watched my husband pull out of the driveway and down the street. Steven, however, responded, "No, he's not. I just saw him leave."

I was confused and questioned him further. He informed me that he was at Richard's, the corner store with a direct view of my house. He had been there for a while, waiting for Terry to leave. I was in disbelief and shock.

After telling Steven that I was headed to bed and hanging up, I couldn't believe my ears when, a few minutes later, he was ringing my doorbell. He had parked outside of my house and was now standing on my porch, knocking and demanding to be let in. Was he now stalking me?

In fear of Steven waking up my children, I immediately opened the door. I exclaimed, "What are you doing? Have you lost your mind? You have to leave now!" The smell of alcohol was strong on his breath as he slurred, "I just miss you." I repeated, "You have to leave now!" He begged to use the bathroom, and in an effort to get him to leave quickly, I allowed him to use the guest bathroom.

While in the bathroom, he continued to beg me to divorce my husband and run away with him. I couldn't believe what I was hearing. "What? Are you crazy?" I exclaimed. Any chance of us being anything was now ruined. The nerve of him to show up at my house like this. I finally convinced him to leave, but the memory of that night would stay with me for a long time.

As he stepped out on the porch, I immediately locked the door behind me, I couldn't help but feel a sense of relief wash over me. I thanked God once again for His grace. However, my sense of peace was short-lived as the doorbell rang again. It was Steven, yelling through the door and peeping through the kitchen window, explaining that his car was stuck in front of my house.

You see, the city of Mobile was working on a drainage repair on my street, where all of the asphalt had been stripped down to just the red dirt. Because it had rained earlier that day, the red dirt had turned into mud, wet and not fit for the weight of a car. Steven's car had sunk right into it, in front of my house.

Despite the uncomfortable situation, I couldn't just leave him there. With my impaired thinking, I jumped into my car, hoping to nudge his car just a little to get him out. But that little nudge became a lot as my car too got stuck, and the rear tires were just spinning, spitting out mud. Fearful of being caught, with our cars bumper to bumper and drenched in red dirt, we had to call a tow truck.

Once the tow truck arrived, I told Steven that he had to pay for my vehicle to be pulled out of the mud, since he caused this big mess. Watching from the front window, with my house doors secured, the truck pulled Steven's car out of the mud and began to drive away. But, as I asked "What about my car?" I feared having to explain to my husband, Terry, why my car was stuck in the mud and moved from the driveway. I eventually had to call another towing company to release my vehicle.

Angry and upset, having spent my last seventy-five dollars to pull my car from the mud, I refused to speak to Steven again. I almost called his wife, but I was afraid of the repercussions.

A few days had passed, after receiving several calls from Steven that I allowed to go unanswered, Terry and I were having friends over as we often did. We were playing the couples' newlywed game when the doorbell rang. Terry dashed to answer it and in walked Steven, disrupting our room of entertainment. My friend, Virginia, was with him. She began to speak to everybody and introduced him as her guy friend.

Looking like I had just seen a ghost; I was in disbelief. My boyfriend was standing in my house, giving dabs and shaking hands with my husband and our friends. Into the kitchen, I grabbed Virginia and she stated, "Steven wouldn't leave her house unless she got in contact with me, and since I was not answering the phone, he made her come over." Nauseous now, I couldn't believe what I was seeing. This was an incident turning into an accident, and somebody would be hurt in the midst of it.

After everyone was gone, Terry began to speak of Virginia's new man, asking me questions regarding him. Well, I pleaded the fifth, I knew nothing about Virginia's new man so I couldn't say anything about him. This was an incident that had turned into a mess, and I couldn't help but wonder how it would all end.

Monday night came and to my surprise, Terry stayed home instead of going out like he usually did. He spent the evening watching Animal Planet, as he often did when he was home or before heading to the clubs. Was this a new Terry? Had my prayers finally been answered, or was he becoming suspicious?

I was deep asleep when the loud ring of the telephone woke me. Terry answered, and the caller hung up. This cycle repeated two more times before Terry asked, "Do I recognize the 251-343 number that keeps calling?" As I lied and said, "No, I have no idea who that could be," Terry dialed the number back. He spoke to a woman on the other end and asked her why she was calling and hanging up. She explained that it was not her, but possibly her husband. Terry asked if her husband worked at Bedero Price, the construction company where Steven and I worked. She confirmed that he had.

With a heavy heart, Terry told her, "I believe your husband is seeing my wife." She responded, "I don't doubt it." After a few more words, Terry hung up the phone.

I had never seen such hurt on a man's face as I did when I looked at Terry. He walked lifelessly into the bathroom and locked the door, preventing me from entering. Through the door, I pleaded with him, apologizing and explaining that I had stopped seeing the man who had no regard for our marriage. Terry stayed in the bathroom for hours, quiet and unresponsive to me.

Earlier, when I had started cheating, I didn't care about Terry's feelings. But now, as I saw the pain I had caused him, I couldn't bear it. After he finally came out of the bathroom, we hugged, and that night our lovemaking was more powerful and passionate than it had ever been. I thought that we could make love and everything would go away. But I soon realized that sex is not a cure for infidelity. It's not a remedy for pain, just a temporary band-aid until the bleeding starts again.

We were fine for a while, but eventually, Terry's cycle of staying out late and coming home just in time to dress for work resurfaced. Our arguments increased, but so did my relationship with God. I had recommitted my life to Christ and was working even more in the church. Even though our marriage was not where I had hoped it would be, I trusted God to fix it, but I never asked for his will to be done.

Terry and I had a very bad argument one night, but this time he left home to stay with his father. He began to do this frequently, but Ms. Mamie, his father's girlfriend at the time, would not let him. She was one of the sweetest ladies I'd ever met, and she always had my best interests in mind. Our spirits recognized each other when we met, and she became the God Mother I never had. I could call her at any time, and she always had a shoulder to cry on when I needed it. Ms. Mamie would call me whenever Terry went to his father's and say, "don't worry, I'm sending him back, just hold what you got!" Unfortunately, Ms. Mamie and Terry's father relationship did not last, and now, after a few weeks of running to daddy's, there was no one to send him back home to me. This time, Terry was gone for good.

A few weeks later, on a Friday night, Terry came by the house, and we made love, and I remember him saying, "I miss my wife!" That was all I heard as he pierced my soul with sexual pleasure. Because my husband was present, I felt whole again. He kissed my forehead before leaving, leaving the wetness from his lips as a sign that he would be back soon. Anxiously, I went to the salon the next day for a new back together again hairdo when my son calls, "Mama, guess who is moving in on our street?" Who was Jarred, I asked. "Terry, and Pops is assisting him." I was riding my bike when "I saw them and asked, and he said, this was his new house now." My mouth dropped to the floor. "Tonya, baby girl, he's gone this time!"

said Ms. Mamie as I called to investigate. "How did he miss his wife last night? But today he's moving into a house on our street?" "Yes, with his girlfriend," Ms. Mamie says. How could he? How could my husband move five houses down the street and become my neighbor with his girlfriend and her children? This was completely disrespectful, an insult, and embarrassing. Why did he come last night? What was his stance? This pain was almost unbearable. It was bad enough to know my husband had a girlfriend, but it was even worse to see her every day as I drove home from work, came in from the grocery store, she passing by, and the two together.

Why, Lord, am I being subjected to such a punishment? I mean, I was in church now, all in for Christ, working in ministry, and leading youth, but my heart was breaking. I was so desperate for the pain to go away that I went to Showers of Blessings Church for noonday prayers and my own church for early morning prayers. I'd feel good in church but then come home to misery. "Where are you, God?" Hell was now encircling me! "He was apparently no longer with me!" "It was clear that God had abandoned me, just as my husband had!" So, there was that Lortab bottle right there, as the devil encouraged me to take every pill and die. On the floor, pushing, screaming, fighting the death demon that was seconds away from possessing me, God showed me my sleeping children. He showed me my only reason for living: my children. He gave me hope by showing me my children in their beds. I began to invoke Jesus' name, pray aloud, and rebuke the enemy who was attempting to devour me. This desperate struggle can only be understood by a mother! I sat at the foot of my bed, staring into the mirror, where it appeared I was having an out of body experience, after getting up from the floor in tears, weak from my battle with Satan. As I reached under the bed where I was sitting to grab a perfectly folded white towel (how did it get there?) and began to wash myself, the Lord spoke to me and said, "I am washing you." I recall seeing myself wash my face, arms, and chest.

I was present in that room, but I wasn't there; it was as if I were on the outside looking in at myself. Terry, he said, "no longer existed to me." "He's dead to you!" he exclaimed. You have been healed, and I have chosen you for a reason." I died on that day! The little girl who had craved attention since elementary school had found love in a savior who would never abandon me. After my death, my life changed. See, prior to death, I was my own worst enemy. I continued on my own path. God had plans for me, but I needed to get out of the way. You must understand that in order to live, you must be willing to die. God had been calling to me, but I had been ignoring him. To see his face, I had to meet my end. My near-death experience cost me my life by resurrecting me.

As I sat in the salon chair, my new stylist, Abra began to examine my hair. "I need to clip your ends," she said, as she gently ran her fingers through the strands. I knew she was right when explaining, over time, as my hair had grown, the ends had become damaged and split. If left untreated, these splits could travel up the hair shaft and damage the roots, leaving my hair dead and lifeless.

Just like my hair, my spirit had also undergone a growth process. I had been spiritually fed, grown in my faith, and worked in ministry, but even as I prayed and sought to better myself, there was damage in the roots of my being. It was only through God's healing and restoration that I was able to truly overcome and move forward.

In the darkest of moments, when all hope seemed lost, God showed up and restored my life. And I know that He can do the same for you. He is a God of second chances and new beginnings. Trust in Him and allow Him to heal and restore you from the inside out.

"God raised Lazarus after he had been dead for three days. If God can do that for him, why wouldn't he do it for us; this can only happen when you totally surrender. To totally surrender may mean it happening when your back is against the wall. It may even happen at a point where you've hit rock bottom. Just know, if God will show up at death for me and raise Lazarus from the dead, he can meet you at rock bottom or against that wall. He is the same God of yesterday, tomorrow and forever more. If he allows you to come so close to death that you can feel it but it does not pierce you, just know that death was for purpose. God will allow that form of contact so that he may get the glory through your purpose!

CHAPTER 10

Pick a Side

As I worked a tight schedule, juggling my job as a glazier for Mobile County Public Schools during the week and my role as an overnight weekend auditor at a hotel in Saraland, I struggled to also maintain my spiritual pursuits as a divorcee. I had my head buried in the word, yet still felt the need for healing. Without fully realizing it, I carried scars from my past relationships and had not taken the time for the seeds of faith to take root and manifest in my life.

One thing I should have learned from my past decisions is that I never allowed God to fulfill his plans for my life before I chose other distractions. But as the All-Mighty, God always finds a way to make his plans known.

As the cold December winds blew outside the hotel, shaking the glass doors and causing me to jump in fear, a man named Carlos walked through the doors. Apologizing for catching me in the act of catnapping. I tried to hide my fatigue as I checked him in. The only available room had a broken heater, but Carlos was willing to accept it at a discounted rate.

As we chatted, Carlos noticed the big black book with red writing on my desk and asked what I was reading? As a new Christian, I began to impress him and myself with my knowledge of the word of God. Perhaps there had been a spiritual growth in my life that I hadn't recognized.

Time flew as we sat and passed the time discussing the word of God until my shift was over. This chance encounter with Carlos made me realize that perhaps God had been working in my life, even when I was unaware.

As the weeks passed, my schedule of working as a school maintenance personnel during the week and an overnight weekend auditor at a hotel in Saraland had me stretched thin. Despite this, I continued to operate in Ministry, seeking healing and understanding in the Word of God. However, my past experiences as a divorcee had left me with deep-seated scars and a lack of clarity about God's plan for my life.

From that night on, Carlos visited me every weekend during my shifts. He was a complete gentleman, always arriving in his navy-blue overalls or denim jumper, steel-toed boots, and white Hanes T-shirt. He explained that he wanted to make sure I was safe overnight at work. As we spent more time together, our Bible study sessions decreased and Carlos would often fall asleep on the loveseat in the hotel's lobby while I finished my paperwork.

His presence had a positive impact on my work environment. Prior to Carlos' visits, I was regularly harassed by drunken men propositioning me for cheap thrills. But with Carlos by my side, these occurrences dwindled. I was grateful for his protection and support, and as our friendship grew, I couldn't help but wonder if there was something more between us.

Over the following weeks, Carlos began to visit me at my home. These visits turned into weekly sleepovers, despite my involvement in the church as a minister and youth teacher. Despite my uncertainty and fear of committing sin and separating myself from God, I found myself drawn to Carlos. Each time we were together, the nudging of the Spirit reminded me of the fornication I was committing. My own selfish desires overpowered my intuition, which I knew deep down to be the Spirit of God warning me. The Bible's instruction to flee fornication holds weight, as engaging in sexual immorality can lead to entangling and intertwining of souls that God never intended. As a form of protection and boundary, God intended sexual intercourse to occur solely within the confines of marriage between a husband and wife. Carlos and I were not married.

As the weeks passed, I allowed Carlos to move in with me. Our relationship had transitioned into a casual, cohabiting one, where we were essentially "playing house" without committing to the traditional expectations of marriage. This lifestyle of "getting the milk for free without buying the cow" became our norm.

Latonya M. Whitehead

As we began attending church together, my inner spirit began to stir with discomfort. I was not fully healed from past relationships and was not ready to engage in another one. Despite this, I found myself caught up in the routine of going to Bible study on Tuesdays, choir rehearsal on Thursdays, and church every Sunday. I sang and praised alongside the congregation, feeling the energy of the Holy Spirit as the musicians played sanctified hits that turned the entire church into a dance party.

But amidst this religious routine, I couldn't help but question my true spiritual state. I was a habitual churchgoer, dressed in my Sunday best and putting on a facade of sanctity, yet my relationship with God felt distant. I found myself not praying as much, and the long talks and intimate moments that I once shared with God felt like a distant memory. Had I left Him again for another relationship? Had I left Him for Carlos?

As I delved deeper into my spiritual journey, it became increasingly clear that one of the fundamental principles of being filled with the Spirit is to maintain a pure and holy body. The Bible teaches that we are the temple of God, and that his Spirit dwells within us. Therefore, it is imperative that we do not defile our bodies with anything unclean, as it is written in I Corinthians 3:16-17, "Do you not know that you are a temple of God and that the Spirit of God dwells in you? If any man destroys the temple of God, God will destroy him, for the temple of God is holy, and that is what you are."

I found myself at a crossroads, grappling with the realization that my actions were in direct conflict with my spiritual beliefs. For a year, I had been lying to myself and indulging in the sinful desires of fornication, but now the Spirit within me was beginning to stir, urging me to make a choice. Just as it is impossible to continue consuming food without eventually feeling the need to regurgitate, it was becoming impossible for me to continue down this path of spiritual dissonance.

I struggled with this internal battle, oscillating between moments of spiritual euphoria and feelings of being spiritually disconnected. It was a constant reminder that I needed to make a decision and commit to living a life that was in alignment with the principles of my faith. I could see the Paul in me, as he spoke in Romans chapter 7:14- while fighting with temptation by saying, *"So the trouble is not with the law, for it is spiritual and good. The trouble is with me, for I am too human, a slave to sin. I don't really understand myself, for I want to do what is right but I don't do it. Instead, I do what I hate. So, I am not the one doing wrong, it is the sin living in me that does. And I know that nothing good lives in me, that is my sinful nature. I want to do what is right but I can't. I want to do what is good but I don't. I don't want to do what is wrong, but I do it anyway. But if I do what I don't want to do, I am not really the one doing wrong, it is the sin living in me that does it. I have discovered this principle of life- that when I want to do what is right, I inevitably do what is wrong. I love God's law with all of my heart. But there is another power within me that is at war with my mind. This power makes me slave to the sin that is still within. Oh, what a miserable person I am! Who will free me from this life that is dominated by sin and death? Thank God, the answer is in Jesus Christ our Lord."* So now, I hope you get a clear picture; I really wanted to obey God, but because of my sinful nature I had become a slave to the sin.

God had not given up on me yet, and over time, I began to feel disgusted with who I had become. I looked and felt like a fraud, a perpetrator, disguised by Sunday church services, suits and pantyhose. I could no longer pretend to be the self-righteous, judgmental hypocrite that I had become. As I eased back into proper placement with God, it was nothing like I had anticipated. I was not forced to redeem myself, all I needed to do was ask for forgiveness and it was immediately granted.

But my past actions had consequences. Carlos and I had decisions to make. I told him, "Marry me or you have to leave." I presented him with the fear of loss, and he ultimately decided that marriage was our best option. However, he was not ready for marriage and I was still carrying baggage from my first marriage, keeping me in bondage. I needed Carlos to make me look better to others, to show that I was capable of loving again, especially to my ex-husband who still lived on my street as my neighbor. But in the end, I realized that true healing and self-worth cannot be found in another person, but through my relationship with God.

On the next Friday, Carlos arrived with a wedding ring set and, on that Sunday, we were wed in my Pastor's study. I remember very little about the details of that day, but one thing that stands out in my mind is the ceiling fan, spinning wildly and making a terrible knocking sound as it rotated. It caught me off guard as I watched it, wondering if it would fall to its final destination, right on top of our Pastor's desk. Despite this distraction, we focused on our vows and committed ourselves to each other.

As newlyweds, Carlos and I were assigned to lead the Youth Ministry at our church. This was a time of great joy and fulfillment for us as we poured ourselves into the lives of young people, helping them to develop their talents and overcome the challenges they faced. I remember driving the church van around the community, gathering youth for Sunday School and church services. It was like being the "little mother in the shoe" with so many children to care for, but we loved every moment of it.

A few months after, we decided to buy our first home. We searched for the perfect house and finally found it; a four-bedroom located at 5616 Moffatt Road. With my approved credit of ninety-eight thousand dollars, we were able to buy it. The sellers paid the closing cost and we only had to pay three-hundred eighty-six dollars for closing fees. Moving into that house was a proud moment for us, it was our first home together, and we had accomplished it as a married couple. This new home purchase fueled my adrenaline for what was to come. We were a power couple on a mission, and our marriage continued to grow stronger every day.

It was a bright and sunny day when Carlos took me to Bay Minette to purchase a brand-new vehicle. A white 2010 Ford Expedition Limited Edition stood gleaming in the showroom, and I couldn't believe my eyes. This was the first time in my life that I had a brand- new car that smelled new, without the blue tree air freshener hanging from the rearview mirror. I felt like the Lord was truly blessing us. We were operating the youth department at the church, had just bought a new house, and now, a few months later, a new car. Carlos had even purchased a Ford F150 in addition to my hunter green convertible Mustang I previously owned. We had all these material possessions, yet we were not consistent tithes payers.

As Malachi 3:8 states, "Will a man rob God? Yet you are robbing me. But you say, 'How have we robbed you?' In tithes and offerings." We were living like The Jeffersons, "moving on up!" But our blessings were short-lived. Carlos was laid off from his job, and our financial strain began to take its toll on our marriage. I was the only one with an income, and our lifestyle was designed for more money than the seven hundred forty dollars I brought home bi-weekly from my job with the maintenance department of the school system.

In the beginning, Carlos would leave early in the morning to look for work, but there were times when he would lie around sulking, possibly feeling sorry for himself. At that time, he needed a wife, a prayer warrior, someone to intercede on his behalf. But all I could see was the bills piling up and his lack thereof. We had placed ourselves in a position to be broke or devoured. Without following the principle of sowing and reaping, we had opened the gates to our capital punishment. We ignored what the word of God said about giving, although our pastor's preached it. Did we not believe that one day we would be held accountable for our actions? Did we think we could continue to live our lives robbing God? There is a price to pay for disobedience, and we were soon to face our judgment day.

It wasn't long before we began to receive the disheartening letters of disconnections, repossessions, and foreclosure. Like many selfish believers, we found ourselves saying, "Oh God, where are you" and "Lord, please help us!" We were now closet praying day in and day out, noonday lunch praying, and even calling on friends for prayer. We were so desperate that it didn't matter to us that we were only soliciting God when we needed him to come through. Were we just using him to get us out of our rut? It seemed that we had reverted to calling on him out of convenience. Whatever our reasons were, we could no longer see God and I could no longer hear the voice that had spoken to me during my rebirth process.

Faced with hard times, I was willing to do almost anything to save my home and my lifestyle. I started by going to the local title pawn store and selling the title to my Mustang, with the hope that next month, I would retrieve it but I only had enough to pay the interest. Then I tried doing odd jobs to get extra money. I was doing cash advances and even attending to an elderly lady three days a week for two hours a day, for eighty dollars. I also took the little foot tub sold in the local Walmart and made appointments for people to wash, clip, trim, paint, and massage their feet for twenty dollars an hour. I found myself hustling trying to make ends meet and keep that roof over our heads.

Finally, after about three months of barely hanging on, robbing Peter to pay Paul, and borrowing from anyone who would lend, my husband got a job. Thank God! The job was in Portland, Oregon, and the company was going to fly him out on a small contract and supply him with room and board, along with a daily meal per diem. All of this sounded great, seeing that we had been receiving foreclosure notices and our time to pay was limited as well as our resources. So, off to Portland, my husband went. However, after a week, Carlos was on his way back home, calling me from the airport stating, "the contract was over." To make matters worse, they withdrew the money for his flight to get to Portland and back home again from his check, leaving him with just fifty-five dollars. "What!" "This cannot be happening!" He misunderstood the entire job assignment. The contract he agreed to was only for one week and the company did not pay for transportation to or from the location. I was furious! This job was a waste of time and money, in addition to his lack of a sense of urgency to stop the creditors from calling. I was hustling by myself; besides, I was the one with three mouths that depended on me for a meal, and later it would be proven.

Carlos had once again received a call from the same company, offering him a three-month assignment. Although he would have to pay for his own transportation, the most cost-effective option was to take the bus. The company covered his

Greyhound fare, but deducted the cost from his pay each week in installments until it was fully reimbursed. In addition to sending money home on a weekly basis, Carlos and I were still struggling financially. We were facing challenges such as the repossession of their vehicles and foreclosure letters from attorneys. This was a difficult period for our finances, and we felt as though we had no other options but for him to be employed away from the family.

As a family, we navigated these financial struggles, I remembered one particular evening when I picked him up from the bus station. We returned home and I began to take care of his laundry while we enjoyed a family evening with our children. The next day, our son Jarred was selected to speak at church, and Carlos helped him prepare. However, as I was folding laundry in their bedroom, I heard a ringing sound coming from Carlos' dresser. Upon searching for the noise, I discovered a small flip phone hidden in the third drawer, with a flashing message notification.

At the time, cell phones were still a relatively new technology, and many companies offered promotions such as "My Favorite Five" which allowed customers to select a certain number of people to talk to without incurring additional charges. Upon opening the phone, I saw a circle of names on the screen, including "Mom," "Wife," and "Latonya" (flashing in red), with two blank spaces remaining. When I confronted him about the phone and the unfamiliar name, he remained silent and refused to answer my questions.

The discovery of the hidden phone and the mysterious "Latonya" left me feeling confused, hurt, and mistrustful of my husband. The ongoing financial struggles and this new revelation added further stress to an already difficult situation for the family.

As the rain beat against the rooftop and the front door, thunder and lightning directly overhead, the rage that had begun to fuel my body was hot as burning coals. His ignoring me had only made matters worse and I was fighting mad. Enraged with fury, I ran to the kitchen, pulling out trash bags and loading his clothes from each drawer, snatching and grabbing everything he owned in those black hefty bags. I was so mad that I was talking aloud to myself while throwing him out, not caring that the children were right there listening.

A few minutes had passed when I heard the front door open. Going to inspect who had come in, I saw that it was Carlos leaving. I paid him no attention as I continued to grab the suits and shoes from the closet and stuffing them into the trash bags, while yelling and screaming profanities to my lying, cheating husband who had no regard for his wife.

After a while, I realized that Carlos had left on foot in the pouring rain. Eager to know who and how he had left, I jumped in the car to see if he was in the neighborhood. After circling a few blocks, crossing Moffatt Road, I pulled into the parking lot of the BP gas station and there he was on the pay phone in the rain. Was this woman that important that he ignored his wife? Did she mean that much to him that he walked in the rain to respond to her missed call? Yelling from the car, I told him to have her pick him up, and that his clothes would be on the porch. I then drove back home, entering the bedroom, dragging the heavy bags to the front of the house to make them more accessible, while also securing the door with the deadbolt lock where he had no key.

In my bedroom, now cleaning up the mess I had made from my fury, I could hear Carlos at the front door demanding me to let him in. Being the immature adult that I was, I ignored him, just as he had ignored me earlier. The kids began to ask, "Can we open the door?" "Don't touch my door!" I responded. Why were they concerned about him being in the rain, besides he was the bad guy, whose side were they on? He was the one hiding a second phone and cheating on his wife, their mother!

And I thought Superman was the only one who could leap tall buildings in a single bound. But no, Carlos could also. Out of nowhere, unexpectedly, he leapt through the bedroom window, scaring us all, asking me, "Where is my cell phone?" My response was, "That's our cell phone. We are married, what belongs to you also belongs to me!" As a way of control, I refused to give him the phone. I never understood why since I had no access to bypass the security code on it. All I knew was that he had the nerve to be talking to a woman who had the same name as mine!

Carlos grabs the keys to the car and drives away, taking nothing but the clothes on his back and not returning for the rest of the night. My condition was restless, paranoid, tossing and turning, wondering where he was, what he was doing, and with whom he was doing it. I began to call the hospitals to see if he had been admitted. I even called the county jail to see if he were arrested. Was this my fault? Had I been a bad enough wife for my husband to cheat on me? Was I the wife that David spoke of in the book of Proverbs 21:9, *"For it is better to live on a corner of a rooftop than share a house with a quarrelsome wife."* To answer my own question, yes, I had become that wife. It was my responsibility as a Godly woman to speak the truth to my husband in love while remaining honest and direct; however, the shock of the situation at hand caused immediate pain and reopened old wounds. I acted out the pain and became a foolish wife, not wise in the least. Even now, when I think about it, I am embarrassed by how I behaved in front of my children.

The following day, I tried repeatedly to reach Carlos to find out where he was, but he was not responding. I was left with no choice but to call the church van to pick up the kids and me for youth service. After church, when we returned home, Carlos was there and had cleaned up the remaining mess. He then informed me that he had called the job back and was going out on another contract, leaving that very night at 8 PM. I was in disbelief, but I decided to let things be. We never discussed the phone incident, and I put it back where I had found it. We were both exhausted and didn't want to fight any more. The kids had already witnessed enough. So that night, with very little conversation, I drove Carlos to the bus station, where he departed once again for a six-month contract. We had agreed that he would come home once a month for a weekend to be with his wife and family, or I would visit him. Satan is tricky and thrives on division, but unfortunately, neither Carlos nor I were able to recognize the division he was causing in our marriage.

As Carlos was returning home after a grueling three-month work assignment, I eagerly awaited his arrival. But as I sorted through the bills that had piled up on the kitchen island, my excitement turned to shock and betrayal. Among them was Carlos' cell phone bill, and upon closer inspection, I discovered an extensive list of numbers from Oregon.

Curiosity getting the better of me, I began to call each number, particularly those with unusually long talk times. To my dismay, many of the calls were from women, and it soon became clear that they were not just acquaintances, but rather individuals with whom Carlos had been unfaithful.

I felt a range of emotions: hurt, anger, betrayal, and devastation. I couldn't believe what I was hearing, as each woman shared their prospective place in Carlos' life. I didn't know how to face Carlos or handle the situation. I felt embarrassed and ashamed, and I couldn't shake off the feeling that it was my fault for allowing him to take the job out of state. I blamed myself, the devil, and even God for what had happened.

I was emotionally drained, heartbroken, and full of self-contained rage. I struggled to rationalize my feelings and justify Carlos' actions. I couldn't understand how he could do this to me and our family. As the reality of his infidelity set in,

Latonya M. Whitehead

I couldn't help but wonder what the future held for our marriage.

As a divorcee, one would expect that I would have grown and learned from my past experiences. However, the truth was that my wounds had not fully healed. It was time for me to mature and put an end to my impulsive reactions. It was time to move beyond childish temper tantrums and start acting like an adult. Although I was capable of consuming solid food, my reactions to life's challenges remained unchanged. The Bible described this phenomenon as double-mindedness and instability in James 1:8. My struggle was spiritual, yet I was allowing my emotions to control me, instead of the other way around. To overcome spiritual battles, one must be equipped with the proper armor, otherwise, they will never win the fight. The world teaches us to never take a knife to a gun fight and the word of God says, *"Put on every piece of God's armor so you will be able to resist the enemy in time of evil. Then after the battle you will still be standing strong. Stand your ground, putting on the belt of truth and the body armor of God's righteousness. For shoes, put on the peace that comes from the Good News so that you may be fully prepared. In addition to all of these, hold up the shield of faith to stop the fiery arrows of the devil. Put on salvation as your helmet, and take the sword of the Spirit which is the word of God (Ephesians 6:13-17 NIV)."* You see, maturity and growth go hand in hand and the key to achieving both lies in the word of God. Despite my own personal growth, I had yet to fully mature. I was still grappling with spiritual immaturity and God was working on me, but it was going to take time and lessons to overcome it.

Like many of us, I learned my hardest lessons the hard way and often had to repeat them before the lessons finally took root. While I was not at fault for my first husband's infidelity, I was at fault for my reaction to it. I failed to fully process the hurt and pain from my first marriage and instead moved straight into a new relationship, hoping that it would heal the wounds left by the first. But as I soon found out, the enemy's work is never done and I was faced with the same struggles once again.

The path to maturity and growth is ongoing, with bigger challenges lying ahead after each victory. The most important relationship one can have is with the Lord, and it is essential to maintain this relationship and continue to seek his guidance, even when it may not seem like he is showing you anything. The one constant thing in this journey is to keep following the Lord no matter what.

CHAPTER 11

Make Something Happen

Lisa was Carlos' girlfriend, or so she believed. She shared with me the details of their meeting at the strip club where she worked every night, and how they would spend the night together before he left in the morning. They would also go on breakfast, lunch, and dinner dates, and spend time together shopping or watching movies in his room until it was time for her to return to work.

However, when I revealed my true identity as Carlos' wife, Lisa was just as shocked as I was. Carlos had told her that he was a single man without children, but the truth was that he was married with five children, as I include my own three. Outraged by his deceit, Lisa and I devised a plan to catch him in the act. We arranged for her to call the house phone at ten PM, and I would answer and pass the phone to Carlos. Our goal was to see the expression on his face and expose his lies.

Lisa had nothing to lose, as he was my husband, but we put our plan into action.

Arriving home, Carlos greeted the children as they prepared for bed, engaging in his usual routine of talking to them about the Bible or telling them an encouraging story before heading to the shower and getting ready for bed. As the two of us lay in the quiet darkness, the elephant in the room was palpable. We tried to engage in conversation but no words would come, no small talk would develop, and silence had taken over our marriage. That was until the telephone rang, exactly at ten o'clock pm. Lisa was on the other end, as planned, asking to speak to Carlos.

Handing him the phone, Carlos was in shock and tried to evade the call or pretend it was a wrong number. However, I went to the kitchen and picked up another phone, calling him out once again for his deceit. With no denial, Carlos hung up the phone, leaving Lisa on the other end.

As I entered the bedroom, Carlos was sitting on the side of the bed in the still, dark room, speechless. He had been caught in his web of lies and was struggling to find a solution. But instead of facing the consequences of his actions, he chose to book a trip back to Portland, the location where he had been caught cheating. This was his way of fixing things, or so he thought. He made the arrangements with his job and left the next day, without a trace.

A month went by with no word from Carlos. I tried calling him but his cell phone was either disconnected or he had changed the number. I was left with no choice but to contact his job and inquire about his whereabouts. I was told he was fine and on the job site, but I would receive a call later.

The call finally came and Carlos delivered a crushing blow: "LaTonya, I do not love you and I don't want to be married. You are a good woman, but you should find someone else." With that, my husband was gone, and I was left to pick up the pieces of my shattered life.

I never thought I'd feel a physical pain from heartbreak until the day I heard him confess to no longer wanting or loving me. The air was knocked right out of me, just like being punched in the stomach. That moment marked the beginning of my journey through the five stages of healing.

At first, I was in shock and couldn't believe what was happening. I felt speechless and spent days repeating the same words, "This can't be happening to me." I turned to my friends and family for support, sharing my story and trying to make sense of it all.

But then came the tears and the anger. I was angry at God, asking why He didn't warn me, why He put us together, and why He was punishing me. I even tried bargaining with my husband, Carlos, but he insisted that I was not the problem and that I would be a better benefit to someone else. The thought of being unwanted and unloved consumed me and I felt embarrassed to face the prospect of another failed marriage.

The bills started piling up and the bank was calling for the mortgage note I couldn't produce. Foreclosure was only a few days away and I was struggling to fight the demon of depression. I felt sorry for myself, stuck on a man who couldn't love me as Christ called him to. I was addicted to the pain and didn't understand what love truly was.

But eventually, I had to embrace the fifth stage of healing - acceptance. I couldn't make my husband love me or force him back home. I couldn't work any harder to catch up on the bills that were left for me to manage alone. It was time to gather myself, lace up my shoestrings, use Vaseline, remove my earrings and start fighting. No more pity parties. It was time to let God heal my brokenness and work miracles in my life.

That Sunday, I went to church, feeling the heavy presence of the Spirit in the building. During the service, a sister I knew but rarely spoke to locked eyes with me several times. It was a strange and unexpected moment, as we just stared at each other from a distance without speaking a word.

The next day, I received a call from that sister, inviting me to her hair salon that evening. I was hesitant but agreed, not understanding why she wanted to see me. We worshipped in the same ministry but had never had much interaction. Little did I know, this encounter would be the beginning of a journey that would change my life forever.

I arrived at her job and found, Sister Sandra, wrapping up a meeting with a client. She invited me to take a seat while she finished her work. Once the client left, she asked me, "How are you doing?" I tried to put on a strong front, pretending everything was fine. "Everything is good," I said, "my husband, church, and the youth ministry are all fine." But Sister Sandra was not convinced. "Are you sure?" she asked.

In that moment, all of my emotions came flooding out and I began to weep uncontrollably in her arms. I let out all of the hurt and pain I had been bottling up for months, telling her about my life's reality: I was scared, divorced, feeling unattractive and unloved, heartbroken and struggling to make ends meet. It was a relief to finally let it all out.

Sister Sandra asked me, "How can I help you? How much do you need?" I was taken aback; I had never been asked that question before. I hesitated, not wanting to offend her by asking for too much. But she spoke up, "Would ten thousand dollars help?" I was stunned. All I could do was cry and say, "Thank you Jesus!" I realized that the Lord, who had been silent to me, had been speaking to her on my behalf.

That moment will always stay with me, when I was feeling unloved and the Lord showed his love for me through Sister Sandra. I am still filled with joy and gratitude when I think about it, and I will always say, "Thank You Jesus!"

I remember the day when Sister Sandra wrote that check for ten thousand dollars. The next day, I went to the bank and deposited it with a sense of relief. I was excited to finally be able to take care of my mortgage and other expenses. However, a few days later, I was faced with a major issue. My septic tank had backed up, causing a terrible odor throughout the community. The repair cost was almost four thousand dollars, which depleted the money I had received from Sister Sandra. I regret not having a better understanding of financial management at the time. If I had, I might have been able to repair the house for a quick sale and use the remaining funds to move to a place that was more affordable for me.

Four months later, I was homeless. My children and I had to break into our own home to shower and eat. We used a window that wouldn't lock in my son's room. Despite my partial faith, I trusted that God would make a way, but I was still trying to figure things out on my own. I decided that when my aunt and uncle came to visit, my children and I would leave Alabama with them for North Carolina.

After that decision, I went to meet with my son's coach, Coach Pope. I explained our hopeless and homeless situation, and my plans to leave in two days. I asked Coach Pope to help me break the news to my son because I couldn't do it alone. I felt like a failure as a mother, unable to provide for my children. I was overwhelmed with feelings of pride, shame, embarrassment, hurt, and fear of what others might say. Coach Pope and I cried together, and he even asked why I didn't seek help from the team or the school. But I couldn't bring myself to do it, feeling ashamed of my inconsistent faith as a youth leader.

As I sat down with Coach Pope in his room, I couldn't help but break down and tell my son, Jarred, that we had to leave effective this Saturday. I poured my heart out, telling him about all the poor decisions I had made that had affected our entire family. But as I spoke, I realized that I had raised a man. Jarred looked at me with tears in his eyes, his chin held high, and said, "Mama, I always wanted the opportunity to play varsity basketball with Leflore, but I have to do what's best for my family." I was both relieved and heartbroken to hear these words. For the first time, I realized that my choices had impacted not just me, but also my children and their dreams.

On Thursday night, as I went to choir rehearsal with the girls, I couldn't help but cry at every song. All I could think about was the abandonment, deceit, and disappointment that had brought us to this point. But during the rehearsal, my phone rang repeatedly from an unfamiliar number. I was unsure who it was, so I didn't answer. Eventually, Kala came in and asked me to step outside. She told me that she had called her best friend, Kethia, and told her about our move. Kethia's aunt had a vacant house that she was willing to let us live in, and she had been trying to call me to tell me about it.

I immediately called Kethia's aunt after rehearsal and found out that the house was available for rent. The kids and I went to see it that evening, but it was already dark and we could barely see inside. Despite the uncertainty of what the future held, I couldn't help but feel grateful for this unexpected turn of events.

The next morning, I set out to visit our new home and meet its owner. The house was situated in a decent neighborhood, not the best, but not the worst either. Despite the vandalized windows and graffiti on its walls, and paint-damaged hardwood floors, it was a blessing to have it. But the greatest blessing of all was that not only had the Lord provided this home for us, but that my kids and I could repair it ourselves.

Thanks to my job in the maintenance department of the school system, I had access to discontinued paint colors that were going to be thrown away. I put my skills as a glazer to use and repaired the broken windows with scrap glass, and used a borrowed buffer to restore the hardwood floors to their former glory. All of this was accomplished on the very same Saturday we were planning to move to North Carolina, and on Sunday, we were able to settle into our new home in the Beau Terror subdivision off Wolf Ridge Road.

I can attest that God will never abandon or forsake us. Sometimes we get caught up in trying to fix things on our own, forgetting that God wants us to rely on him so he can guide us. There have been many instances in my life where I've taken the lead, only to be redirected. God wants to change the trajectory of our lives and make our future years better than our past, but he needs us to be willing participants. By stepping aside and letting him take the reins, he can heal, deliver, and set us free.

CHAPTER 12

The Cheat Sheet

My kids and I have finally found our footing in our new home. Balancing work, managing bills, and living frugally, we are content with life. That was until one late night as I sat in front of my trusty old Windows computer, browsing through spam and ads. That's when I stumbled upon a dating site that piqued my interest. I decided to create a profile, complete with a photo and descriptions of my likes, dislikes, hobbies, and location. The next morning, I woke up to an overwhelming response to my entry. I couldn't believe that so many people found me, this "ugly duckling," attractive or interesting.

However, I couldn't help but wonder if it was all just a ploy to ensnare me, especially since I was still dealing with the aftermath of my failed marriage and my insecurities of low self-esteem and the desire for love and acceptance. Despite the notifications from interested men on the Black People Meet website, I couldn't read their messages until I paid for a membership.

With only fifteen dollars to my name, I was faced with a difficult decision. Should I use it for my lunch for the next few days or give in to the temptation of potentially meeting someone new? My past relationships had left me yearning for attention, and I'm sure by now, you have noticed my pattern. In the end, I chose to go with the dating site, succumbing to the anxiousness of what may come next.

I was initially scared to respond to anyone on the dating site I stumbled upon. Despite the convenience of this latest technology, I was wary of the dangerous people who might prey on young women like me. I also hesitated to engage with profiles that featured pictures of luxurious homes, sports cars, boats, and businesses, as I felt I had nothing to offer compared to those comforts. However, one particular guy caught my eye, as he sent me daily greetings without any turnoff messages like "Hey Sexy." Intrigued by this dark-skinned man with a charming smile and white teeth, I finally responded, and we engaged in an eight-hour conversation, which led to more day-to-day interactions.

Over the course of a few weeks, we learned so much about each other through written words, and soon he asked if he could call me. I was thrilled to hear his voice and learn more about him. He was former military turned contractor in Iraq, from a large family in Georgia, much like my own. I shared my story of being separated from my husband and highly active in my church ministry. We became attached, communicating through the webcam and phone, having movie nights and virtual dates. Our love continued to grow without any physical intimacy, and over the next eighteen months, we spent every free moment talking and getting to know each other better.

As I got to know Franklin better, I came to see him as an angel in human form. He began showering me and my kids with gifts and money, without us even having to ask for anything. He was constantly making sure we had everything we needed and wanted, and he would even donate to my church's youth department or pay tithes on occasion.

One particular moment stands out in my mind. I had invited a family of four unfortunate children to spend the weekend with me to attend my daughter's cheerleading competition in Florida. The children's mother was struggling with drug addiction, and they arrived at my house without even basic necessities like clothes, a toothbrush, or a change of underwear. I told Franklin the story, and he immediately sent me five hundred dollars to take the kids shopping. He wasn't just concerned with my well-being, but also with the well-being of the children I was caring for that weekend. He truly was the Boaz that every woman dreams of.

It was July 4, 2010, when I received a call from Franklin asking what my plans were for the holiday. I had no plans, as my children were teenagers and spending time with their friends. But Franklin invited me to join him and his family in Orlando,

Florida, for a trip to Disney World. Originally, we had plans to meet face-to-face on July 10th, but Franklin couldn't bear the thought of waiting another week to see me. In a rush, I started packing my bags, but I was worried about not having anything to wear besides old rags. But Franklin reassured me, saying, "Just come, don't worry about clothes. I'll take care of you." And he did - not only did he buy my plane ticket, but he was also willing to take care of me in every way.

As I embarked on my journey to Orlando, I was filled with a mix of excitement and nerves. It was my first time flying and I was awestruck by the sheer number of people surrounding me at the airport. I had a layover in both Atlanta and Charlotte and during my time at the airport, I found myself frantically running through the terminal, dodging crowds of people, in my attempt to make it to my gate in time.

Finally, I arrived in Orlando and called Franklin, who was to be my host for the weekend. As I stepped out of the airport and made my way to baggage claim, I anxiously awaited our reunion. When we finally embraced, I felt a slight tingle, but to my disappointment, it wasn't the same passionate love I had felt from a distance.

We made our way to the Timeshare where Franklin's family was staying. As I entered the room filled with strangers, I felt like an outsider, with very little welcoming from his family. Franklin introduced me as his friend, LaTonya, but the under-the-breath murmuring from some of them made me feel uncomfortable.

Latonya M. Whitehead

Despite the lackluster start to the weekend, I made some new acquaintances, including one of Franklin's nephews and one of his friend's wives. They made an effort to make me feel more at ease, but as the night went on, I couldn't shake the feeling that the weekend wasn't starting off as planned.

We all had a nice dinner together after leaving Disney World, and the family began to question me, which was to be expected. After dinner, I assumed we'd all be living in the same house, but Franklin had other plans. He had arranged for us to stay in a hotel room separate from the rest of the family. When we arrived at the room, I was nervous and afraid, and I felt butterflies that made me think I needed to relieve myself in the bathroom. Running into the restroom without locking the door, Franklin enters naked a few minutes later, as I sat on the commode defecating. The man I'd been talking to for almost two years had me in a precarious position. I couldn't get up; I was stuck on the toilet, pleading with him to leave the restroom, but he wouldn't! He kept rubbing his hands through my hair and on my face, around my lips, grabbing the back of my head, and forcing me to kiss his body while I sat there relieving myself! I was disgusted and humiliated! I knew he could smell the bile that eluded the bathroom but he just acted like an animal in heat, touching me and forcing his nature upon my mouth, gagging me with unconcern as I engulphed swallowing his penetration, then being left to privately wipe and clean myself, getting into the bath to shower with lowliness, meekness and shame; hinging onto that same demon that molested, raped and over powered me at five, and in middle school. Only this time, I felt trapped, because this demon had been providing for me, showering me with gifts and the lifestyle I had only imagined, but never had and always desired.

From that day forward, I was putting my body, my integrity, and my relationship with God at risk for the man who began paying my bills, supplying my needs, sending gifts of new computers, refrigerators, shopping sprees, vacations, furniture, and so much more in exchange for sex tapes, recorded moments of masturbation, and requested minutes of disgrace to myself by sharing nude pictures with him from a distance via computer. I'd lost myself in the world of selling my body for money. This soul connection with him had me craving chump change for pictures and videos of my most valuable commodity (my body). Without ever standing on a street corner, I labeled myself as that harlot, or prostitute, willing to sell her soul to the devil via the internet.

In the beginning, God created woman as a prize and a gift to man. He declared that it was not good for man to be alone and therefore made a helper for him (Genesis 2:18). Unfortunately, many women, including myself, struggle with recognizing our worth as a gift. Trauma often leads to denial and a lack of self-acknowledgment, causing us to settle for less and accept scraps in exchange for our bodies.

As I open up my own journey, I pray that my transparency will reach other women who have also used sex for money or allowed it to control their lives. The man I spoke of earlier was supplying my needs, but Philippians 4:19 says, "But my God shall supply all of your need according to his riches in glory through Christ Jesus." This means that God's resources are limitless, and he wants us to have faith in his ability to provide for us.

It's important to remember that we are a gift from God and should never compromise our bodies, integrity, or relationship with him for anything less. We are not streetwalkers or prostitutes, no matter what label society may put on us. Instead, we are beloved children of God, worthy of love and respect.

Continuing in my disgrace of fornication and harlotry for another three years, Franklin rerouted our trip, deciding that we would leave Montgomery together and visit a friend of his in Augusta, Ga. When I arrived at this house of inertia, I wondered who lived here because of the lack of activity, automobiles, and dormancy. He entered with a key and led me to the living room, where the furniture was still covered in price tags and plastics. "Where is your friend?" I wondered, raising my suspicions. "Whose place is this, really?" He proceeded to tell me, "This is your house, I bought it for us, will you marry me?" "What!" To my surprise, had all of my dirty trashy videos finally paid off? Was being so provocative and sexually promiscuous for money now worth it? Those were the questions that later occupied my mind as I said yes to another man and marriage, when the ultimate question should have been, was God pleased, and was this his desire for my life?

Despite my reservations and misgivings, I said "yes" to a man who did not truly hold my heart. I was drawn to the idea of stability that he offered, but not the man himself. He lived in a foreign country, and his lack of preparedness to lead left me feeling uncertain. His questionable morals, including his devotion to a Masonic thirty-third degree, only added to my hesitations. He would frequently disappear for weeks at a time to attend sabbaticals or meet with his secret society, leaving me to wonder about my own well-being. Despite my lack of physical attraction to him, I agreed to marry him for the promise of financial stability, hoping that love and attraction would eventually follow.

In March 2014, after a romantic weekend getaway, I made the decision to move to Georgia and start my new life with my husband. My children had all grown up and moved out, and I was ready for a change. Our wedding was a private affair, attended only by close family and friends, held in South Carolina to maintain a sense of intimacy. The first few days of our marriage were filled with excitement and happiness, but that quickly faded when my husband had to leave for work in Kuwait, leaving me alone for another six months.

During his absence, I enrolled in college and took on a job as a manager at a local dollar store chain. I was finally living the lifestyle I had always imagined for myself, shopping and traveling on weekends, treating myself to weekly hair and nail appointments, dining at fine restaurants, and impressing my friends on Facebook. I had no worries and felt that this was the path that God had intended for me.

Latonya M. Whitehead

Separated by distance, we were not the typical union but still a loving marriage. Now it was time for another-six month visit where Franklin would stay home in the states for two weeks. This particular vacation was one where we spent in Hawaii. It was wonderful, living on the beach and fine dining. You see, whenever Franklin came home, it was always a vacation for us, we would travel visiting new places I had never seen; those trips led us to Vegas, California, Atlantic City, Louisiana, Washington, Hawaii, and many other places until that simple drop off to Atlanta's airport.

Over the course of two years, my daughters Jaz and Kala had moved to Georgia with me. Kala, a flight attendant based in Dallas, Texas, had two children and frequently traveled the world for work. Jaz and I would take care of the kids during her absences. One day, after a vacation with my husband Franklin, he was scheduled to depart from Atlanta's Hartfield-Jackson Airport. On the way to the airport, Franklin asked to use my phone to log into his Facebook account and post some pictures from the trip.

However, after Franklin insisted that Jaz and I head back to Augusta rather than wait for his takeoff, Jaz discovered a series of disturbing messages on my phone, which was still logged into Franklin's Facebook account. The messages showed that Franklin was expressing his desire to sleep with another woman and they were sending each other explicit pictures. This realization came as a shock to me, especially since I had compromised my own values during our dating process by sending explicit images to Franklin.

As I drove back to Augusta with Jaz and my grandkids in the car, I was filled with anger and frustration. I wanted to call Franklin and confront him about his disrespectful behavior, but I had to remain calm and composed in front of the children. The two-hour trip felt like four hours, as I struggled to contain the fiery emotions inside me.

As I arrived home, I couldn't help but continue to read the messages my husband had been sending another woman on Facebook. I confronted him about it, but he quickly logged out of his account and we ended up getting into a heated argument. I was so hurt and angry that I refused to speak to him for weeks, until he sought guidance from our pastor and I reluctantly decided to answer his calls. Franklin apologized profusely and promised to never disrespect our marriage again. Despite my doubts, I foolishly trusted him and we continued what I thought was a fulfilling and loving union.

The following year, I was determined to advance in my career at the dollar store, but there were no opportunities for growth. I began searching for other employment and eventually landed a job as a store manager at a convenience store chain. I loved my new job, but I was ambitious and wanted to achieve more. After discussing my aspirations with my bosses, I was offered a promotion as District Manager with a company car, pay increase, and thirteen stores under my supervision, all located on Washington Road in Evans. Our long-distance marriage was working well, but everything came to a halt after a visit to the doctor.

During one of my husband's home vacations, we decided to take a short beach trip to the Outer Banks. We stayed in a small rental home and spent our days fishing on the pier and eating at local restaurants. It was a quiet and relaxing vacation for us, as we usually went to places where casinos and gambling were readily available. However, this time I wasn't feeling well and was relieved that we didn't engage in our usual activities. On the trip, I started experiencing a burning sensation and pain when urinating. We quickly got AZO tablets and cranberry juice to try and fight off what we thought was a urinary tract infection. Despite some relief, we still headed back home so Franklin could prepare to leave for his next deployment. But just two days later, my symptoms worsened and I was forced to visit Fort Gordan's military base. I wasn't diagnosed with a urinary tract infection, but I left the hospital with antibiotics.

My husband was days away from me and I had just found out that he had been unfaithful again, this time without even using protection. The betrayal was devastating, especially considering the numerous times he had cheated in the past. I couldn't even begin to recount all the instances in this book.

As I sat in the doctor's office getting an antibiotic, I couldn't help but wonder if this was all my fault. Had I made a mistake by choosing financial security over love? Was I getting what I deserved for going against my instincts and saying yes to a marriage that felt wrong in my heart?

The pain only worsened when my husband denied having any diseases and sleeping with someone else. I had remained faithful and yet, he had the audacity to lie to my face. My mind played tricks on me, making me believe that it was just a freak accident. It wasn't until months later, when I received phone calls and messages from women on Facebook, that the harsh reality hit me.

Despite the knowledge of my husband's infidelity, I found myself unable to leave. I loved him and the stability that came with the marriage. I loved being able to spend money freely, go on lavish trips, and live a life of luxury. I didn't want to go through another divorce and I hoped that this phase would pass.

My husband's declarations of love, accompanied by beautiful gifts, only reinforced my belief that everything would work out. It wasn't until much later that I realized that I was the true gift in this relationship, one that couldn't be bought with money. I should have been valued and treated as a precious and rare diamond, worthy of honor and admiration.

Four months had passed, and Franklin and I were determined to make our marriage work. Despite my insecurities and lack of communication, I had thrown myself into my job, working hard and striving for success. That hard work paid off when corporate offered me a relocation to Charlotte, North Carolina - a place I had visited with Franklin and whispered, "I could live here." It seemed like God had intervened, and a month later, we sold our home in Georgia and temporarily moved into an apartment until we could find a new home to buy. I saw this as an opportunity to start our marriage anew, and with the promise that 2018 would be Franklin's last year living abroad, I was eager to finally live together as husband and wife.

I set about finding the perfect home for us, with just one month to prepare for Franklin's arrival over Labor Day weekend in 2018. I threw a family celebration, inviting both of our families to come and enjoy the festivities. Sadly, only Franklin's mother was able to attend from his side, but my entire family came up from Alabama, along with my aunt Freda and Granny who lived just a couple of hours away. The weekend was filled with good food, laughter, and love. My uncle Dobie took on the role of grill master, and as he likes to think he is a philosopher after a few drinks. Franklin appeared to be overjoyed with our new home, which was fully furnished with all new things, including a pool table in his mancave. He even had a framed jersey of his favorite team, the New England Patriots, and a set of pool balls to match. It was the perfect start to our fresh new beginning.

There was enough space for everyone to sleep comfortably in the house. The kids took the man cave, where they slept head to-head on the sectional and floors, just like in my own childhood. Franklin and I had the comfort of our bedroom while the other spaces and guest rooms were filled by the rest of our guests.

But that peaceful sleep was disrupted when Jaz, who was sleeping in the man cave, found a cell phone that was buzzing with message notifications throughout the night. When she opened the phone, she realized it belonged to Franklin and was filled with messages from a woman.

The next morning, I was stunned and angry when Jaz showed me screenshots of the messages. Franklin was telling this woman that she was the best he had ever had in bed and he couldn't wait to get back to her. I felt a mix of disbelief and fury. I refused to cry this time, as I had in the past, instead feeling numb and determined to confront Franklin about his lies and deceit.

As soon as everyone left on Sunday morning, I showed Franklin the phone and confronted him about the messages. But to my disappointment, he tried to deny the truth even though the proof was right in front of us. This was the turning point in our marriage and I realized that I had no more energy to fight for this hopeless situation.

I want to share with you my story, not as a guide to leaving your marriage, but as a reminder that you deserve better. I stayed in my marriage for far too long and I want to encourage you to seek God, rewind the footage of your relationship, and determine if you are making the right moves.

God wants to provide you with security and love, but we often distract ourselves with other things and become impatient with His plan. We think we want a quick and easy solution, but God's plan for our lives is never about microwave blessings. Just like it took the Israelites forty years to leave Egypt, we too must trust in God's plan for our lives; it just may take longer than we expect it.

I was captive in my own life until I had my mind renewed. As I share my story, I hope that you can assess your own damages and use my experiences to help heal your own heart. God is faithful and will guide you through the journey of heartbreak and renewal. This book is my cheat sheet to a better life and I hope it can be yours too.

After dealing with the emotional turmoil of a potential separation from my husband Franklin, I was faced with the reality of seeing him again when he returned home for a vacation in February 2019. It had been two months since we had last spoken, aside from a brief conversation on his birthday the previous January. Despite the tensions between us, we had already made plans to celebrate Mardi Gras in Alabama with his family, and we decided to follow through with these plans, pretending to be a happy couple in front of his family.

Upon our return to Charlotte, the next two weeks were filled with tension as we struggled to come to terms with the damage done in the months following Franklin's unfaithful episode. I had forgiven him, but I no longer respected him as my husband, and I was determined to leave him as soon as I had enough savings to support myself.

However, one night, while I was working in bed, Franklin approached me, trying to start an argument. I tried to ignore

134

him and focus on my work, but he persisted, insulting me and accusing me of infidelity. Fed up with his accusations, I told him to leave me alone. This only made him angrier, and he lunged at me, striking me in the mouth and attempting to choke me. I managed to escape and run to the bathroom, shouting, "It's over. I will never let anyone lay their hands on me again."

That night became a turning point in my life. I left my home after Franklin struck me. I sent a text to my daughter Kala from the bathroom, waking her up from sleep. I informed her that I was gathering my belongings in a duffle bag, preparing to leave. Unbeknownst to me, Kala secretly made calls to my son, Jarred and daughter, Jaz, explaining that my husband, Franklin, had hit me.

As I was packing, I could hear Franklin's phone ringing in the background while we were arguing. When he finally answered, it was my son on the speaker asking, "Did you hit my mama?" Franklin's reply was a shocking, "I just wanted to rough her up a little!"

Jarred, showing his manhood, firmly stood up to Franklin and told him that he would not allow anyone to harm his mother. Meanwhile, I called Franklin's mother, hoping that she would scold him for hitting me. However, to my disbelief, her response was merely to advise him to not hit me where it could be seen.

These events only reinforced my decision to leave and never return. The fear of Franklin's PTSD potentially hurting me in the middle of the night was too great to ignore. I quickly packed and left with Kala and my daughters, leaving the home I had worked hard for behind.

I had no plans of ever looking back. All the lessons God had taught me throughout my life finally resonated. I trusted in His plan and obeyed His will. I was uncertain about what my future held, but I knew without a doubt that God would not leave me. I didn't know what my friend circle would look like after I left or what the other side of letting go would bring. I didn't care about Franklin's version of the story. All I knew was that God would take care of me.

Dear reader, as you embark on this journey with me, I would like to encourage you to let go of worries about tomorrow and embrace the power of trust. Trusting in the Lord is a gradual process that requires effort and patience. However, if you take the first step and trust God with the small things in your life, you will soon realize that the bigger things are just a mere challenge for him.

I stand as a testament to the truth that the Lord is indeed faithful. When you put your faith in the Almighty, he will demonstrate his love and power in your life in ways that words cannot express. The Lord is not just present in your life, but he actively shows up and makes his presence known. He is there to provide comfort, guidance and strength when you need it most.

So, I encourage you to open your heart to the Lord and allow him to work his supernatural power in your life. Trust that he will never abandon you and that he has a plan for your future that is beyond what you can imagine. The Lord will show out for you and the experience of trusting in him will be life-changing.

CHAPTER 13

I am that Dummy

December 18th, I had a business meeting with my company and a local tobacco brand. After the meeting, a man named David approached me, introducing himself as a territory representative for my stores. During the introduction, David stated, "LaTonya I've been looking for you." After a brief investigation, it turned out that he had been dialing the wrong number. Despite the mix-up, David was polite and walked me to my car, making sure I was safe from oncoming traffic before opening my car door for me.

During our conversation, David expressed an interest in discussing my stores and their sales performances in greater detail. We agreed to meet again and he suggested that we set up a calendar invite via email. Three days later, we met at a local Panera Bread for another meeting. Over the course of six hours, our conversation expanded beyond business and turned personal, touching on topics such as our marriages, beliefs, and relationship histories. I was impressed with David's honesty as he shared his struggles with infidelity and the challenges, he faced in trying to repair his broken marriage.

Despite being married, David and I grew closer over time, enjoying lunch and dinner dates, concerts, cookouts, movies, and sporting events. We were both happy to have a close friendship and didn't seek anything more. Our past relationships had left us both burnt, and we were content with just being friends. That year, I had secured a six-figure net income, giving me financial independence and the ability to take care of myself without relying on a man.

As my estranged husband and I began the official process of separating in North Carolina, my relationship with David was evolving into something neither of us had anticipated. Both of us were hesitant to become too invested in a commitment, as I wasn't truly ready to settle down with any one man. I was excited to finally experience my newfound freedom, and I was confident in my own abilities, feeling that I did not need a man to define my self-worth or to make me complete.

David, too, had moved on, finalizing his divorce and securing a townhouse, which he had generously given me a key to. But one night, after a particularly intense day, David and I found ourselves at odds and I chose to stay at my own home instead of spending the night at his, where I had been residing for weeks. However, due to a migraine, I was unable to rest and so I returned to David's place, in the hopes of finding some relief.

Upon arriving, I found the garage open and the house unsecured. As I made my way upstairs, I noticed that the bedsheets had been removed and changed, and there were burning candles on the dresser. My personal belongings in the shower and bedroom had been discreetly stored in a closet, out of sight. This was all too familiar to me, as the familiar scent of dishonesty filled the air.

As I reclined on his brown leather couch, I found myself in a state of contemplation. I weighed the options of whether or not to call him, or to allow him to enter into the surprise of my presence. In the end, I decided to send him a simple text message, stating "you left in such a hurry, you forgot to close the garage." He replied by asking "where are you?" and I couldn't resist the satisfaction of bursting his bubble as I replied, "I am at your place!"

David arrived home, having retrieved an item belonging to his female companion from the kitchen drawer, which he promptly took to her car. After she left, David returned to the house, but I was left with many questions, despite knowing the answers, I asked them anyway. I needed to understand why my things had been moved, why the linens had been changed and concealed, and whether his night of play had been interrupted by a lingering headache that forced me to make the four-mile journey back to his place after leaving.

As I stood in the kitchen, I became introspective, reflecting on past experiences with men and realizing that this decision was critical and permanent. I questioned my motives for my friendship with David. Was I seeking financial luxuries, a romantic tryst, or something deeper? I was determined to make the right choice, as David asked, "What are you doing?" I replied, "David, I am making sure that when I leave, I do so with certainty, with no plans of returning."

Although we were enjoying a friends-with-benefits arrangement, our lives would never be the same. I was drawn to David, not only because he possessed a piece of each of my former husbands, but because he embodied the best of all three of them. He was the perfect version of them, and I didn't want to leave him. I was able to be my authentic self with David, sharing my fears, embarrassments, and tears without fear of judgment or misunderstanding. We both sought solace that night, covered in blankets and reclining on the couch, where we slept until morning.

As the sunlight streamed in through the mini blinds, David and I arose and decided to go to church. I set off for home to freshen up, then headed to a local church that we had picked randomly using Google - The Ashley Church. However, upon arrival, we were disappointed to find that the parking lot was full, forcing us to park down a nearby street. The quarter of a mile walk back to the church was uncomfortable for me as my toes were beginning to poke through the peep-toe of the heels I was wearing, causing me to limp in agony.

The Ashley Church was a fascinating experience, packed with a large and diverse congregation of people from different nationalities. We were so impressed by our first visit that we continued to attend the church for three more Sunday services. We also had the opportunity to have lunch with the assistant pastor and his wife, as well as participate in the annual church cookout held at the youth pastor's home. Unfortunately, our time at The Ashley Church was cut short as the Covid-19 pandemic swept across the nation, causing the closure of churches, schools, businesses, and any public social gatherings.

During this time, I had moved in with David, leaving Kala and the girls at the old house as the separation proceedings continued. Once the divorce was finalized, Kala moved into her own apartment as well. David and I were now living in his two-bedroom townhouse, with my furniture in storage and my winter clothes in his garage. We quickly realized that this living arrangement was not sustainable for us if we were to continue our now monogamous relationship. Hence, we decided to buy a home and began looking at different neighborhoods and developments every weekend.

One of the places David took me to was Olmstead. The sight of a quarter of a million-dollar homes there made me dream of a life of luxury. I wanted to experience the opulence of a five-bedroom, four-bath home with a basement, butler's pantry, living and family room, privacy fences, covered patios, decks, and swimming pool.

Riding with David on Saturdays was a nostalgic experience for me. It reminded me of my childhood when my mother would take me on drives through affluent neighborhoods. We would sit in her car in the middle of the street and admire the beautiful homes, their well-manicured lawns, and the elegant fixtures and fittings. These rides with David allowed me to dream again. I saw visions of things that seemed impossible to attain, and it reignited a fire within me.

As we drove through these neighborhoods, I couldn't help but contrast them with the reality of my own life, living in the duplex on Montgomery Street in Prichard, surrounded by rats and roaches. My vision of life had been distorted by years of abuse and hardship. But as my perspective cleared, I came to believe that I could have everything that God had promised me. I decided to trust in my Father and let Him give me what I deserved. And God used David to remind me of that.

After a difficult battle with my ex-husband over the home we purchased together, I decided to let him have it. I realized that holding onto the past and clinging to the wrong people and things can prevent me from entering into the promises of God. I had to let go of my own feelings, thoughts, and emotions and embrace what God had planned for me. Even though I had lived a life of sin, God's grace and mercy covered me.

In the book of Philippians, chapter 3:13, Paul reminds us to forget the things that are behind us and reach forth to the things that are before. We cannot successfully walk into our future while looking back and clinging to our past. I had to learn that lesson the hard way, but through it all, God's love and mercy sustained me.

As David and I embarked on our journey to find a place to call home, we formulated a plan to improve our financial standing and increase our credit score. Our perseverance and patience were finally rewarded when we discovered The Oaks at Skybrook. This new development in the Huntersville community was a blank canvas waiting for our imagination to bring it to life, and we were approved for a home worth over four hundred thousand dollars. Despite the challenges posed by the ongoing pandemic, we eagerly awaited the call from the Design Center to select the materials that would transform our dream into a reality. We meticulously chose every aspect of our home, from the door handles to the countertops, from the roof to the flooring, from the lighting fixtures to the faucets, and every detail in between. We envisioned it, wrote it down, and gave it to God, and He brought it back to us.

In our lives, we must grasp a fundamental truth: the acts of God do not require our cooperation. God does not need us to help Him accomplish His plans. All He asks for is our surrender. To truly grow spiritually, we must understand what God is doing and simply get out of His way. On January 28th of the following year, David and I closed on our new home, realizing that God had fulfilled His promise to not withhold any good thing from us. Although the topic of marriage had been discussed between David and I, we were in no rush to solidify it and preferred to take our time. David would often say, "We shouldn't continue living in a manner that goes against our values and beliefs."

On February sixteenth, after a long day of work, David surprised me with a pampering session at the local nail salon. I was so tired that I fell asleep in the pedicure chair. Later, as we were heading home, David pre-heated the oven using his phone, and together, we enjoyed a delicious dinner that he cooked. I was just settling in for a quiet evening at home when David played some of my favorite music, and we danced and sang together. It was a magical moment when David pulled out a stunning pear-shaped diamond ring and proposed to me. I was overjoyed, and I still remember the expression on his face as he asked me to be his wife.

David and I were now engaged, and we were looking forward to our wedding on July third, just five months away. I was slowly decorating our new home, which was almost 3400 square feet, while balancing my demanding job as a district manager. My job had become increasingly stressful due to the challenges posed by the pandemic, including mask-wearing robbers, staff shortages, school closures, and a lack of applicants for open positions. I was working almost 16 hours a day and was suffering from migraines, which had sent me to the emergency room three times in a month. Despite these difficulties, I did everything in my power to support my store managers, even working overnight shifts at the registers to keep the doors open. Despite my best efforts, my bosses seemed unsatisfied, and I was struggling to balance everything.

Latonya M. Whitehead

On March 9th, after being overwhelmed by stress and suffering from constant headaches, I came home to a heated argument with my partner, David. He was worried about the impact my job was having on our relationship and my overall health. I was so busy with work that I often relied on unhealthy snacks for all my meals and was unable to take care of myself properly.

That evening, as I went to my closet to change before showering, I suddenly felt an outpouring of tears and called upon the name of Jesus for guidance. As I fell to my knees, I felt the presence of the Holy Spirit calming my spirit and speaking to me in a language only he could understand. The Lord then commanded me to resign from my job, which was a difficult decision for me as I had always been self-sufficient and was afraid of becoming dependent on someone else. However, I realized that it was the Lord who had always taken care of me, not my job.

With this newfound clarity, I turned off my phone and sent an email to my bosses resigning from my job, effective immediately. After taking a shower and wiping away my tears, I sat down for dinner with David, who informed me that he was considering ending our wedding plans. I listened to his arguments and concerns, until finally, I revealed that I had just quit my job. David was taken aback and seemed to have a weight lifted off him as well. The next day, I collected my belongings and company car and officially ended my time at the job.

Reflecting on the sequence of events, it is clear that life can take unexpected turns. My plan to unpack my new home and plan our wedding was disrupted when David called me from work, suffering from intense lower back pain. Despite my efforts to provide pain relief, the pain persisted and we took him to the emergency room. Unfortunately, his injury left him unable to work and with no source of income.

Adding to the challenges, we had just closed on our house with a mortgage of $2600 per month, and I had resigned from my job a few weeks earlier. The prospect of losing our home and possessions was very real, and the added stress of planning a wedding only added to our anxiety. However, in the face of adversity, we found strength in our faith and relied on God to direct and provide for us.

We chose to be good stewards of what we had, prioritizing giving and tithing even without a consistent paycheck. My husband, being the head of our household, made it his daily practice to pray and listen for God's guidance in all decisions. I, too, sought guidance from God in my closet prayers, to fulfill my role as a helper to my husband. Together, we trusted in God's plan for our lives and were ultimately rewarded with a beautiful wedding on July 3, 2021, a union that we give all the glory to God and his son Jesus Christ. Through our story, we hope to inspire others to surrender their lives to God and experience his grace and blessings.

As the saying goes, "you can learn a lot from a dummy." I, myself, am that dummy, and through sharing my story, I hope that you will see yourself in me and learn from the lessons I have learned. During a time of unemployment, David and I turned to God, asking for His guidance and provision. This is what true surrender looks like - not just a concept, but a reality based on personal experience. It is this type of surrender that captures the Lord's attention.

With maturity and wisdom, we made sure to prioritize our giving, even when we didn't have a steady income. Paying our tithes and being good stewards of what had been given to us was our first responsibility. Instead of putting tithing on the back burner, we made a conscious effort to continue giving and planting seeds wherever we could. My husband, as the head of our household, made sure to keep his steps ordered by the Lord and made giving a priority. Our story is one of being sinners saved by grace, and our goal is to empower others while giving all the glory to God.

CHAPTER 14

Identity Theft

The title of this book is "I Got Issues:" A Journey of Faith and Healing," inspired by a powerful story found in the Gospels of Matthew, Mark, and Luke. The story took place in the town of Samaria, where a woman struggled with a persistent issue - a blood flow that lasted for twelve consecutive years. Despite seeking help from numerous doctors, her condition remained unmanageable.

However, the woman heard about Jesus and his miraculous healing powers, and so she made her way to the place where she knew he would be passing through. With a deep sense of urgency, she fought her way through the crowd, declaring her hope that if she could just touch the hem of Jesus' garment, she would be healed. The woman knew the power of Jesus and believed that she needed little else to be made whole again.

Latonya M. Whitehead

As Jesus walked through the crowd on his way to heal Jarius' son, the woman reached out and touched the hem of his garment. Her touch was so powerful that Jesus instantly recognized the strength of her faith. In the midst of the crowded mob, he stopped and asked, "Who touched me?" Her touch was different from the rest, and Jesus immediately healed the woman, making her whole again.

This story is a reminder that when we recognize and respond to the presence of Jesus in the midst of our struggles, we invite the supernatural into our negative circumstances. The woman's touch was a testament to the power of faith, and Jesus' immediate healing is a testament to his love and compassion. As believers, we can learn from this woman's example and find the courage to reach out and touch the hem of Jesus' garment, inviting the supernatural into our lives and finding healing and wholeness through our faith.

I am intimately familiar with the struggles of a woman who has faced multiple issues in life. Just like the woman mentioned in the Bible who struggled with a menstrual flow problem, I have faced a multitude of difficulties that have left me feeling lonely, broken, and deeply wounded. The experiences I have gone through have had a domino effect on my life, including being subjected to abuse, infidelity, and exploitation. I have struggled with low self-esteem, depression, and feelings of neglect and insanity, compounded by traumatic experiences such as molestation, and rape.

At a young age, I found myself struggling with my own identity. The traumas and difficulties I faced had left me feeling like I was nothing more than what had happened to me. I was constantly searching for love and approval in all the wrong places, trying to fill the void with temporary fixes like changing my appearance or seeking relationships with others. Despite my efforts, my problems continued to haunt me, leaving me feeling trapped and unable to escape. I was left with deep scars that ran deep, and I felt there was no hope for my situation.

In this book, I share my personal story of overcoming these difficulties and reclaiming my identity. Through my journey, I hope to provide encouragement and guidance for others who may be facing similar struggles, and show that it is possible to find healing and hope, no matter how broken and defeated one may feel.

I can relate to the woman with the menstrual flow problem because I, too, have struggled with my own issues. Like her, I have felt lonely, broken, and hurting on the inside. The Bible only mentions her one issue, but can you imagine dealing with multiple problems at once? Her one issue led to her being trapped by others. Despite seeing countless doctors and depleting her finances, she not only still had an uncontrollable blood flow, but also developed low iron deficiency.

Similarly, I have faced my own struggles including abuse, infidelity, low self-esteem, neglect, depression, and even sexual assault. These experiences led me to lose sight of my true identity, and I allowed myself to be defined by others. I tried to fix myself through superficial means such as changing my appearance and seeking validation from others, but these temporary solutions only left me feeling empty and hopeless.

My issues continued to haunt me, weighing me down and preventing me from finding relief. I felt stuck, just like the woman with the menstrual flow problem. It wasn't until I had a few spiritual deaths and rounds of insanity that I truly understood that God had chosen me and that I was chosen to carry burdens, heartache, disappointment, and loss before triumph. It was difficult, but through suffering and torment, I learned to set boundaries and recognize my purpose. God had to allow my world to be turned upside down in order for my test to become his testimony. I am grateful for the opportunity to cheat death until his will is done.

I am willing to share my story, to reveal every detail, the good and the bad, without holding back. I am not afraid of the consequences that may come with the truth, such as gossip, disapproval, or even being ostracized. I embrace this challenge and refuse to let shame and guilt control me. This book has set me free, inspiring me to write and speak my truth, just as my struggles led me to seek comfort in Jesus. The pain I have experienced has urged me to pray in the middle of the night and to embrace my scars, knowing they can serve a purpose. God blesses authenticity, not the person I pretend to be, but the person he created me to be.

Let's learn a few things about the woman who had the blood problem. Over two thousand years ago, when a female was on her menstrual cycle, she was considered unclean, and people would separate themselves from her. Can you imagine having no friends, no one to talk to, and being cast out of her own society for twelve years with a constant blood flow? She was unable to attend dinner parties, weddings, or even have anyone celebrate her birthday. Can you imagine how lonely she had to be? She wasn't dating, and she didn't have a boyfriend or a husband. In fact, if she was bleeding for twelve years, we know she couldn't have children during that time. Do you understand what it's like to be that lonely? Do you know what it's like to be alone? When my husband left, I felt that kind of loneliness. It was a pain of mourning and grief for the dead that cut to the core of my being. The kind of pain that kept me sitting in cold bath tubs, sobbing uncontrollably with a towel wrapped around my face so my children wouldn't hear me cry. The kind of agony that drove many people to slit their wrists or jump in front of a train to end it all. This lonely pain was like a cancer, eroding my inner flesh and concealing the residue behind smiles and a phony image. Only God and time could bring this pain to an end.

This lady had been suffering from this constant blood flow for twelve years. As I previously stated, not only did a lack of blood cause iron deficiency, but her visits to various doctors in search of a cure cost her money. She was desperate enough to try anything and anyone just to be normal again. I can relate once more. My problems were so traumatic that I needed to be healed from within. I became engrossed in simply surviving, pretending to be fine, never truly recovering, learning to survive but never learning how to be healed. This caused my cycles to last much longer than they should have. I had to lower my -self dignity by talking vulgarly on the phone with men just to get forty dollars from them to pay my water bill. I hide my face in shame when I recall the times when that one would pull into my driveway on a monthly basis to satisfy his fetish, earning him the nickname Nipple Man, in order to pay my light bill. Every time my husband left, I was left in charge, and in order to maintain control, I would concoct any old remedy. Prior to knowing Christ, I felt compelled to do whatever it took; however, after revelation, God became my Savior and true hope for my family.

God created man first in the family and made him the head and leader. When a man leaves his family, he abandons his responsibilities. Consider the relationship between the head and the body: the head, with the brain inside, directs every limb of the body. The hand is told when to wave, the legs when to walk, and the stomach when to eat. Without the head leading and instructing, the body cannot function properly and may be in a post-coma unresponsive state. This is similar to what happens when a man abandons his family. God holds the man accountable for the failure of the foundation of the house, the body, the wife, the children, and so on. This failure can become a generational curse, but a strong woman, even in her worst conditions, can rise up with tenacity and strength to keep the house together. Despite broken blinds, dying flowers, and cobwebs in the corners, the house will still stand because of her sacrifices. God created us to face adversity in our development process, and He was with us even when we didn't recognize Him. Through our trips, falls, and fumbles, He made sure we got up.

As the Lord directed me through the writing of this autobiography, he reminded me not to be ignorant of Satan's schemes. He showed me that the enemy will intensify his efforts as this book reaches a wider audience and begins to bring healing to others. The Lord instructed me to remain steadfast in my faith and not be swayed by false rumors and distractions. He told me that I may lose people along the way, but not to chase after them, as this book and my purpose have nothing to do with them. He promises that every life this book touches will see the results of victory. You may think you are reading just my story, but in reality, this is our story. Through every tear, every note you take, every prayer and conversation about this book, God will deliver, heal, and set you free from your struggles. You may not struggle with a blood dysfunction, abandonment, or low self-esteem, but rest assured, your creator knows your struggle and has the solution.

You are not holding this book and reading it by chance or circumstance. It is all by the will of our Heavenly Father. My story has a level of hope, resilience, deliverance, and perseverance as does yours. You must trust God through it all, choosing to swim rather than drown. You must persevere in the face of adversity, knowing that the enemy wishes to keep you from your destination, which is Jesus Christ. Even if the process appears to be slow and unmoving, remember not to rush it. Do not try to fix it yourself with a screwdriver or hammer; instead, call in the professional, Jesus! The solution to your problem may not be visible, but trust me when I say it's marinating in your Father's kitchen, sitting in that seasoning, the longer it sits, the better the flavor. The longer your season (Issue)- seasoning takes, the better you will be!

Because I was caught up in a world of delusion, believing that my way was the only way. It took me forty years to recognize and confess my failings to God. To achieve freedom, I had to be willing to let go of everything and everyone that was a hindrance. I couldn't become who God wanted me to be until I let go of who I was used to being. You, like me, and that woman with issues, must remember your character and know that you are being healed! You must declare with your mouth that you will protect your dignity by not engaging in immoral behavior or doing things that devalue you! You must remember that you are a gem, a prize, and a gift. Please understand that you are an asset, not a liability! The atmosphere shifts when you arrive! People should recognize greatness when you walk into a room! It is critical to know your worth, and never, ever lower your value or settle because they cannot afford you or you are out of their price range. And to the enemy reading, listening, and watching, don't get it twisted: just because we love you does not mean we won't leave you! We have issues, but we will not be subjected to your disrespect, neglect, or abuse. Yes, we have flaws, but we will not let you hurt, step on, beat up, or destroy our esteem! We will never beg for your attention, time, or affection again!

We're done being easily assessed by people who don't prioritize us!

Throughout your cycles, you must learn to stop fighting against who you are, which is fearfully and wonderfully created. You see, you must refuse to accept their inconsiderate treatment of you! You cannot allow others to treat you any kind of way. Stop allowing others to treat your symptoms and instead allow the Holy Spirit to treat the source of your problem. You must stop allowing their folly to interfere with your ability to live! It's time to walk upright now!

Astutely walk with your head held high! Step into your victory! Walk in your victory, knowing that "even if you have issues, you are healed and whole in Jesus' name!"

But they that wait upon the Lord shall renew their strength; they shall mount up with wings as eagles, they shall run and not be weary, they shall walk and not faint.

Isaiah 40:31(KJV)

Though your beginning was small, yet thy latter end should greatly increase.

Job 8: 7 (KJV)

All Glory & Honor to My Lord & Savior Jesus Christ

Amen

www.ingramcontent.com/pod-product-compliance
Lightning Source LLC
Chambersburg PA
CBHW060525130626
46553CB00002B/657